The Decembrist Movement

Russian Civilization Series

Editors

MICHAEL CHERNIAVSKY

IVO J. LEDERER

The Decembrist Movement

MARC RAEFF

Columbia University

PRENTICE-HALL, INC., *Englewood Cliffs, New Jersey*

Prentice-Hall International, Inc., *London*
Prentice-Hall of Australia, Pty. Ltd., *Sydney*
Prentice-Hall of Canada, Ltd., *Toronto*
Prentice-Hall of India (Private) Ltd., *New Delhi*
Prentice-Hall of Japan, Inc., *Tokyo*

Current printing (last digit):
10   9   8   7   6   5   4   3   2   1

Library of Congress Catalog Card No.: 66-11188
Printed in the United States of America
C-19714 (P)   C-19715 (C)

Foreword to the Series

The presentation of Russian history and civilization in this country has been shaped to a significant extent by the absence of adequate original source materials. Linguistic competence in Russian remains today indispensable for advanced training and research. It is regrettable, however, that the majority of students interested in Russia but not in command of the language should be denied opportunities for delving into the raw materials of Russian history.

Our purpose is thus relatively simple: to make widely available important Russian sources and to help remove Russian studies from the realm of the arcane and the exotic. Each volume in the series is designed to present source material on a significant problem of a given period—medieval, Imperial, or Soviet. Each volume, moreover, involves a careful translation and basic annotation so as to be intelligible to the undergraduate or the general reader and of scholarly use to the graduate student, to teachers, and to non-Russian specialists.

The series, spanning both the Tsarist and Soviet eras, concentrates on hitherto untranslated sources. In the main, too, it presents them in full text and without abridgment so as to expose both flavor and meaning in a document, memoir, or treatise. In this the series deliberately differs from the documentary collections usually found in one-volume compendia covering long periods and many themes.

The introductory essay in each volume places the issues and sources in their larger context. The essays are designed to provide guidance to the reader and generate new approaches to the understanding of the distant and recent Russian past.

Michael Cherniavsky
Ivo J. Lederer

Author's Note

All dates are those of the original, i.e., according to the Julian calendar in use in Russia until 1918, which lagged behind the Gregorian calendar by twelve days in the 19th century.

The following titles are given in abbreviated form in the text:

PSZ

Polnoe Sobranie Zakonov Rossiiskoi Imperii (Complete Collection of the Laws of the Russian Empire), 1st series, St. Petersburg, 1830.

Izbrannye proizvedniia Dekabristov

I. Ia. Shchipanov and S. Ia. Shtraikh, eds., *Izbrannye sotsial'no-politicheskie i filosofskie proizvedniia Dekabristov*, Vol. I. Moscow, 1951.

Vosstanie Dekabristov

Tsentrarkhiv—Glavnoe Arkhivnoe Upravlenie, *Vosstanie Dekabristov (Materialy/Dokumenty po istorii vosstaniia Dekabristov)*, Vols. I-XI. Moscow, 1925-54.

The following symbols have been adopted:

( )   translator's and editor's additions

// //   translator's and editor's summary or paraphrase

Marc Raeff

Contents

The Decembrist Movement

I

The Decembrists

December 14, 1825, was the day set for taking the oath of alle-✗ giance to the new Emperor, Nicholas I. Only a few days earlier, on November 27, when news of the death of Alexander I had reached the capital, an oath of allegiance had been taken to Nicholas' older brother, Grand Duke Constantine, Viceroy of Poland.[1] But in accordance with the act of renunciation he had made in 1819, Constantine refused the crown. The virtual interregnum stirred society and produced uneasiness among the troops, and the government was apprehensive of disorders and disturbances. Police agents reported the existence of secret societies and rumors of a coup to be staged by regiments of the Guards; the new Emperor was anxious to have the oath taken as quickly and quietly as possible. The members of the central government institutions—Council of State, Senate, Ministries—took the oath without incident early in the morning. In most regiments of the garrison the oath was also taken peaceably. But in a few units the soldiers were given a chance to

---

[1] As a full description of all the events is readily available in English, only a bare summary will be given here. For a complete chronicle see Anatole G. Mazour, *The First Russian Revolution, 1825—The Decembrist Movement: Its Origins, Development, and Significance* (Berkeley, Calif.: University of California Press, 1937; reprinted by Stanford University Press, 1962).

display their bewilderment at the rapid succession of rulers. Seizing on this mood, some officers, members of a secret society, led about 3,000 men into the Senate Square, where they lined up in combat readiness. The conspirators hoped that this display of discontent and show of force would rally all of the capital's garrison to their ranks. Poorly and hastily planned, inadequately executed, their scheme was frustrated; no other units joined them. The mutineers confusedly waited for orders to act, while their officers merely went about their ranks, encouraging them to stand firm and shout for Constantine.

In the meantime Nicholas prepared his countermoves. He acted cautiously, since he did not feel sure of the loyalty of the troops and overrated the degree of disaffection among the Guards. While the mutineers waited for developments, Nicholas, his brother Michael, and their generals gathered loyal troops, artillery in particular, and surrounded the Senate Square. The Military Commander of St. Petersburg, General M. A. Miloradovich, tried to persuade the mutineers to disband, but one of the conspirators, P. G. Kakhovskii, shot and killed him. Not even the Archbishop could persuade the soldiers to go back to their barracks. Late in the afternoon Nicholas at last felt confident of the superiority of his forces and ordered the artillery to open fire. In a few moments the mutineers dispersed. Within the next twenty-four hours all the leaders of the revolt had been arrested, and the mutinous soldiers disarmed and confined to their barracks. The day which had begun in fear, hesitation, and confusion ended in bloodshed and an easy victory for the government.

In retrospect it is quite clear that the conspirators—known as the Decembrists because of the date of the events—had no chance of success, for their plans had been poorly laid and their leadership was found wanting. Prince S. Trubetskoi, slated to be the dictator, vanished when it became clear that no government dignitaries could be enlisted to head a provisional government. Yet, the government had been greatly alarmed; the very fact of revolt made a deep impression on the country. Before the total victory of the government had been confirmed, rumors spread that the capital was in open rebellion and that the whole garrison had risen against the new Emperor. Reaching the Second Army in the Ukraine in the last days of December, this rumor precipitated another revolt. In the hope of aiding the rebels in St. Petersburg and of overthrowing the imperial regime, the officers of the Chernigov Regiment persuaded their soldiers to start out for the capital. They were stopped by loyal government troops near Belaia Tserkov and easily defeated. An attempt to lead the regiment of Poltava to their defense did not succeed. The revolt in the South collapsed as easily, though more bloodily, as the mutiny in the capital. By mid-January all was quiet again in the Empire, the leaders of the revolt in prison, the mutinous soldiers disciplined.

A Commission of Investigation was appointed to get to the roots of the revolt. The evidence it gathered, consisting of the comprehensive statements made by the Decembrists, was turned over to a special High Criminal Court. On the basis of this evidence alone the Court pronounced sentence. Five leaders were condemned to death and hanged on July 13, 1826, and 121 individuals received various sentences to hard labor, disciplinary battalions, and exile. About 300 more, mainly soldiers and noncommissioned officers, were disciplined and transferred to remote and dangerous garrisons and kept under special surveillance. Thus ended the Decembrist uprising; but this end was only the beginning of its historical role.

The immediate cause of the revolt had been a crisis of succession. Alexander I had died suddenly without leaving any children. In accordance with the provisions of the Statute on Succession and Imperial Family,[2] the throne was to be occupied by Alexander's oldest brother, Constantine. But in 1820, after Constantine's marriage to a Polish noble lady who was not of royal blood, Alexander added a provision for morganatic marriages[3] to the Statute on the Imperial family. Thereupon Constantine formally renounced his rights to the crown in an exchange of letters with his brother; and in 1823 Alexander I gave the transaction legal sanction by a manifesto which, curiously, he kept secret, although Nicholas, next in

---

[2] Dated April 5, 1797; PSZ, No. 17910.

[3] Marriage of a member of the Imperial family to a person not belonging to a ruling house, disqualifying the parties concerned and their children from any claim to the Russian throne.

line of succession, seems to have been apprised of its general tenor.
It still is not known why this vital transaction, which affected the
future and peace of the Empire, was kept in such secrecy as to
create confusion at the crucial moment of Alexander's death. Nor
has it been established whether Constantine's renunciation was
voluntary and whether Alexander considered the settlement to be
final.[4]

It has been suggested that actually Constantine retained the
hope of ascending the Russian throne and that he used his position
in Poland to lay the groundwork for it.[5] As Viceroy of Poland
Constantine was also Commander-in-Chief of the Polish army. His
relations with Polish society were good and he organized his army
efficiently and along relatively liberal lines.[6] Although Constantine
was as much of a drillmaster as his brothers Alexander and Nicholas
(and their father Paul I), he was a more popular figure. His harsh-
ness and occasional brutality were balanced by genuine generosity,
an ability to forgive and forget insults, and great personal charm.
Residing in Warsaw, and in theory subject to the limitations of the
Constitution that Alexander had granted the Kingdom of Poland
in 1815, Constantine was surrounded by an aura of liberalism (which
in fact he hardly deserved). He had brought the Polish army to a
high level of military efficiency, so that the 90,000 men under his
command seemed a power not to be easily dismissed. Had Constantine wanted, he could have laid claim to the throne and backed it
with significant military power. But so far it has not been possible
to determine with certainty whether Constantine seriously hoped
or intended to succeed his brother despite his earlier renunciation.

Another puzzling question is why Nicholas did not act on the
basis of Constantine's renunciation (of which he knew), and why
he disregarded Alexander's specific injunction to learn and obey
the terms of the manifesto of 1823 and Constantine's letters of 1819
before taking any step. Instead, Nicholas himself swore allegiance
to Constantine and forced the reluctant dignitaries to do likewise.

---

[4] Alexander deposited copies of the manifesto and his exchange of letters
with Constantine in a sealed envelope marked, "to be kept and not opened
until I remand it."

[5] S. B. Okun', *Dekabrist M. S. Lunin* (Leningrad: 1962), pp. 65-91, *passim.*

[6] It was almost a "draft army," the length of service being only eight years,
as contrasted to the twenty-five-year service period in the Russian army.

A plausible hypothesis for Nicholas' behavior deserves to be summarized here.[7]

Constantine had earned his poorly deserved popularity and reputation of liberalism mainly because he was far away from the center of Russian public life. At the same time, Nicholas, because of his constant presence in St. Petersburg, had earned a justified reputation as a very harsh martinet. Like his father Paul I and grandfather Peter III, Nicholas was a rigid and ruthless disciplinarian of the eighteenth-century Prussian school. Unlike his elder brothers he had little personal charm, social grace, or political talent to offset the roughness of his personality and his crude barrack manners. Mostly ignored by his older brothers (who were his seniors by seventeen and nineteen years), he had been raised under his mother's guidance in the tradition of Paul's "Gatchina" garrison ways, and his general education had been much neglected. Devoid of imagination and of any conspicuous talents, he was a pedantic, coarse, narrow, and dull person. In the years following 1815, when Alexander I decided to take the army firmly in hand after the wars against Napoleon had produced a relaxation of discipline and a decline of its standard of performance on the parade grounds, Nicholas proved a most exacting and successful drillmaster. But his petty and harsh disciplinary actions earned him the hatred of both soldiers and officers under his command, especially in the regiments of the Guard where he was throughly detested.

The Guards' feelings toward Nicholas were not unknown, of course, to the Military Commander of St. Petersburg, General Miloradovich. Perhaps Miloradovich wanted to play "king maker," perhaps he had a genuine concern for the political stability of the Empire, or perhaps he had some personal reasons. In any case, he painted Nicholas a black picture of the Guards' questionable loyalty; according to Miloradovich, the Guards were not in a mood to accept Nicholas as ruler; and if the latter proclaimed himself Emperor, as was his right and duty according to the dispositions made by Alexander, he would invite open rebellion. In case of such a rebellion, Constantine could easily move on St. Petersburg with his powerful Polish forces and seize power for himself. Milorado-

---

[7] See A. E. Presniakov, *14 Dekabria 1825 goda* (Moscow and Leningrad: 1926), Chap. 3.

vich, therefore, may have persuaded Nicholas to secure Constantine's public renunciation before taking the reins of government. This would account for the interregnum which followed from Constantine's refusal to go along with Nicholas' maneuvers. The confusion deepened and finally led to the very revolt which Miloradovich's counsel had aimed at forestalling and of which, ironically, he was the only victim on the government's side.

The foregoing hypothesis is strengthened by the fact that Nicholas learned of the existence of secret societies and of their plans for radical changes in the regime at the same time that the news of Alexander's death reached him.[8] Nicholas thought the societies' power and influence to be much greater than they in fact were, and noting that many of the leaders were (or had been) officers of the Guards, his apprehension of the Guards' reaction to his enthronement was very great indeed. His fears were increased by the memory of the role played by the Guards in the numerous palace coups of the eighteenth century, as well as in the more recent deposition and murder of Paul I. Nicholas, therefore, was more receptive to Miloradovich's arguments than he would have been had he learned of the true character and strength of the secret societies.

The French Revolution and the Napoleonic wars produced a fermentation of minds which led to an activation of European political thought and life, manifesting itself in the formation of secret or semisecret patriotic and political societies. Russia was no exception to this trend. Partly under the influence of what they had seen abroad during the military campaigns, partly in imitation of local precedents, after 1815 many officers banded together in secret societies dedicated to the promotion of their country's social and political progress. Three of these secret societies were directly involved in the events of December, 1825. In the capitals, St. Petersburg and Moscow, the so-called "Northern Society" was the center

---

[8] Alexander had been informed of the existence of the secret societies through denunciations some time before. But he had failed to take any action on the report, except for approving the investigation that the Commander of the Second Army had suggested. The reason for his passivity is one of the many mysteries that still surround Alexander's personality and reign.

of attraction for all those young members of the educated elite who were dissatisfied with existing conditions and in search of means to change them. During the three years preceding their abortive revolt on Senate Square, the members of the Northern Society were principally engaged in debating what program and tactics they should adopt and in enlisting new members. With respect to the latter, they had not been very successful, for the government's control was quite effective and since 1821 its spies and agents had infiltrated the army. Only the news of Alexander's death and the ensuing confusion resulted in the enrolling of quite a few new members. No full agreement on tactics had been reached, however—hence the society's lack of preparation at the decisive moment of action. There were endless discussions on the desirability of regicide (most members recoiling from it), as well as debate on the usefulness of propagandizing the common soldiers and on means for spreading liberal ideas among the elite. Some members also worked on schemes for a reorganization and reform of the government, the most elaborate, though never completed, being that of Nikita Murav'ev (see IV, b). Their major goals were to bring about personal security, some degree of political participation by the elite, a thorough improvement of all branches of the administration (particularly the judiciary), and some betterment of the peasants' lot. There also had been suggestions to take advantage of a succession crisis (Constantine's renunciation was known in high government and court circles, with which the members of the Northern Society had close links) to compel the Senate to set up a provisional administration headed by well-known and respected dignitaries of the Empire (the names of Speranskii, Mordvinov, and Ermolov were mentioned most frequently in this connection). Until the time this provisional administration could be set up, Prince S. Trubetskoi, head of the Northern Society, would act as dictator. To this end Trubetskoi prepared the draft of a proclamation (see IV, a) and a constitutional project which closely followed the provisions of Murav'ev's constitution. But Trubetskoi lost his nerve at the last minute, and the Society's actions on December 14 were improvised by the more radical and less experienced poet K. Ryleev.

The revolt in the Ukraine had been the work of the "Southern Society," assisted by members of the Society of United Slavs which, in September, 1825, had merged with it. The Southern Society had been activated mainly by former officers of the Semenovskii Regiment who were transferred into the Second Army in the Ukraine after the regiment had been disbanded following its soldiers' mutiny in 1820. The leading spirit and brain in the South was Colonel P. Pestel', a strong and striking personality, whose forcefulness, organizational abilities, and political acumen were allied to a passionate will to power. He had been primarily responsible for the parting of the ways between the moderate Northern and the more radical Southern leadership at a meeting in Moscow in 1821. He then proceeded to create a tightly knit organization of devoted followers and inspired them with the idea that direct action to seize power was necessary in order to bring about a change in the country's regime. On his own admission, Pestel' had been much influenced by the Jacobins in France. His was a mind attracted to comprehensive rational and orderly schemes, as illustrated by his draft of a constitution, the Russian Law (see V, a), in which he worked out in full detail the scheme for a rigidly centralized and authoritarian government. Realizing that the Southern Society would have to use military force to attain its goal, Pestel' and his friends turned their attention to propaganda and indoctrination directed at the rank and file. His energetic and enthusiastic assistant, Lt. Colonel S. Murav'ev-Apostol, wrote the "Catechism" (see V, b) that was read to the soldiers on the eve of their battle with government troops, in which appeal was made to the common people's religious notions and traditions in order to secure their loyalty. Whereas the soldiers in St. Petersburg went along reluctantly and were kept in the dark about the true aims of the revolt, the soldiers of the Chernigov Regiment followed their officers willingly and remained loyal and steadfast even in the face of defeat.

The Society of United Slavs was the creation of some rank-and-file officers from the garrisons of the southwestern border areas.[9] The leaders of the United Slavs constituted the "proletariat" of the Russian nobility: they were poor and had received only a limited education. Living among the mixed populations of the

---

[9] A convenient summary, although by no means adequate study, of the United Slavs is the recent book, George Luciani, *La société des Slaves Unis* (Bordeaux: Université de Bordeaux, 1963).

western borderlands of the Empire, in direct and close contact with the Polish nobility, they had become keenly aware of the multi-national character of Russia, and of the variety among all the Slavic nations. Their nationalism and patriotism, therefore, took on the form of panslavic sentiment. Actually their notions of what constituted the Slavic family of nations were rather vague, since they included the Magyars and omitted the Ukrainians among whom they were actually living. But they were genuinely and deeply sympathetic to the plight of the peasant, in whom they saw the best elements for hope in Russia. They wanted to concentrate their attention primarily on enlightening the peasants and on teaching them through the example of their own lives. Confronted by the aggressive and seemingly very powerful Southern Society (whose representatives exaggerated its influence), the United Slavs agreed to combine with it. Ironically, they had merged with an organization whose centralistic and Great-Russian bent was con-trary to their basic idea of a Slavic federation. Nonetheless they loyally did their part in the battle near Belaia Tserkov.

The Decembrists concentrated on the political reorganization of Russia. They expected such a reorganization to eliminate the worst features of autocracy, improve the administration, and, in so doing provide greater security and scope for the individual educated citizen (primarily the elite, nobility, and some merchants). Although they strongly condemned serfdom and its economic and social effects, the Decembrists did not devote much attention to working out a practical program for eliminating it. Their diagnosis and their somewhat superficial remedies were based on physiocratic notions, with some sprinkling of poorly digested economic liberalism along the lines of Adam Smith. True, Pestel' tackled the question of serf-dom more directly. He suggested complete emancipation, with the preservation of the communal landownership to provide the peasants with a minimum of economic security and prevent their becoming a landless and rootless proletariat. But in other respects, Pestel' con-tinued in the footsteps of eighteenth-century Kameral-und Polizei-wissenschaft, retaining government supervision over economic life whose role he assessed purely in terms of state needs. The Decem-brists' concentration on politics is readily understandable if we remember that they belonged to the upper class, whose economic

position and social status were still reasonably secure. Their conflict with the government was based on their concern for the state's
power and glory and the nation's welfare.

The Northern and Southern Societies were offshoots of the
Union of Welfare, which had been active between 1818 and 1821.
The latter was itself the offspring of the Union of Salvation (1816-
18), of which we know very little and whose constitution has not
been preserved. Both Unions had been organized by officers and
members of the educated elite in the capitals immediately following the campaigns of 1813-14, in imitation of the German patriotic
society, the *Tugendbund,* with which they had become acquainted
in Prussia. As the Constitution of the Union of Welfare (see III, c)
makes abundantly clear, the organization had two principal aims:
moral and spiritual self-improvement of the elite and the enlightenment of the leadership groups in Russian society in order to pre-
pare the ground for social and political reforms. Russia's social,
economic, and political systems were to be transformed as a result
of the gradual and organic work of the members of the Unions of
Salvation or of Welfare. Dissatisfaction and impatience with this
limited and gradualistic approach led to the breakup of the Union
of Welfare and to the constitutions of the Northern and Southern
Societies.

Like the *Tugendbund,* the Unions of Salvation and of Welfare aimed at the country's national and spiritual regeneration.
Such a regeneration was necessary, the members thought, because
the defeats at the hands of Napoleon had pointed up the regime's
moral inadequacies. Such sentiments had become manifest even
before the conclusion of the wars against Napoleon, perhaps even
before the Campaign of 1812. A secret society was organized by
General M. Orlov, who enlisted a handful of members into his
"Order of Russian Knights." Most of them were eventually also
associated with the Decembrist societies, although Orlov himself
withdrew from active participation before 1825.

On the surface, conditions in Russia about 1820 were not any
worse than they had been a decade or two earlier. Why then should
the Decembrists have been so much more wrought up about them
than their fathers or elders? The principal reason is to be found in
the high expectations of the generation that came to maturity on

the eve of Napoleon's invasion. Indeed, it was a sense of disappointment that goaded the Decembrists into action. The reign of Alexander I had opened on a note of optimistic expectation of constitutional and administrative reforms and of the establishment of a firm rule of law (*Rechtsstaat*) which would enable both the individual citizen and the nation to make rapid economic, social, and cultural advances. The hope may have been illusory from the start, for it is questionable whether Alexander I meant to introduce a constitution, although he did wish to improve the administration.[10]

But the educated elite's disappointment did not become acute until after 1815. Napoleon's invasion in 1812 and the campaigns of 1813-15 led the government to make statements that could be interpreted as a pledge of fundamental reform after the war. Constitutions were also promised to the other peoples of Europe who were freed from Napoleon's yoke. After Napoleon's fall constitutional monarchies were established in France and in many German states. Even the truncated kingdom of Poland, in personal union with Russia, received a constitution. Yet nothing was done for Russia. The disappointment and anger of those who had risked their lives to help other nations secure the benefits of constitutional government were great. Russia's glorious role in defeating Napoleon, it was felt, had to be given adequate recognition. Instead, the future Decembrists watched with dismay Alexander I subordinate Russia's national interest to Metternich's reactionary policy. The sense of national pride and dignity had grown and become self-assured during the war, and now, deeply hurt, it could not reconcile itself to the preference Alexander seemed to give foreign interests and foreign-born officers and friends.[11] A few inconsiderate and deprecatory remarks which Alexander I made about his own nation aroused the intense anger of the future Decembrists and contributed to the development of xenophobia among the elite.

The generation of the Decembrists came of age at a time when nationalism was becoming the major factor in European life. It is

---

[10] See M. Raeff, *Michael Speransky, Statesman of Imperial Russia* (The Hague: 1957), Chap. 2.

[11] "Our Tsar—a Russian foreigner," the Decembrist Ryleev wrote in a propaganda poem of the same title; K. F. Ryleev, *Stikhotvoreniia, stat'i, ocherki, dokladnye zapiski, pis'ma,* Iu. G. Oksman, ed. (Moscow: 1956), p. 230.

not surprising that the Russians, too, developed national sentiments to a high degree, especially after they had successfully coped with the French invaders.[12] Little wonder that the Decembrists craved to introduce into public life what they felt were Russia's own historical institutions and national traditions; hence their frequent use of medieval terminology in their constitutional projects and in their memoirs. Peter the Great, they believed, had imposed institutions too closely imitative of foreign models; it was time to return to genuinely Russian form. However, the Decembrists never rejected the spirit of modernity and reliance on Western culture and political liberalism. On the contrary, they felt that the successors of Peter I in the eighteenth century, and particularly Alexander I, had betrayed what was good and genuinely useful in the Western models and imitated only the harmful externals. While advocating a return to old Russian institutions, they endowed them with the ideas and ideals of Western European civilization and liberalism.[13]

The government's lack of respect for the accomplishments of the Russian nation was particularly noticeable in the treatment of the army after its return from abroad. Like all male members of his family, Alexander I had a passion for the externals of military life; he had "paradomania," as Prince Adam Czartoryski remarked. Of course, the war had damaged this aspect of the military establishment. Soldiers who had to fight real battles lost the habit of the perfect parade step and the precision of drill exercises. Zealously assisted by his brothers, Constantine, Nicholas, and Michael, Alexander resolved to restore the Russian army, especially the Guards, to its earlier parade-ground style. This was done with unflagging energy by means of the most brutal punishments and a callous disregard of the health and spirit of the soldiers. Some officers knew no limits in the brutal and merciless treatment to which

---

[12] The ground had, of course, been prepared at the end of the eighteenth century, when the educated elite (in imitation of similar trends in the West?) began to take pride in Russia's cultural accomplishments since Peter the Great and its glorious military medieval past. See Hans Rogger, *National Consciousness in Eighteenth Century Russia* (Cambridge, Mass.: Harvard University Press, 1960).

[13] See S. S. Volk, *Istoricheskie vzgliady Dekabristov* (Moscow and Leningrad: 1958), Chap. 4; H. Lemberg, *Die nationale Gedankenwelt der Dekabristen* (Köln-Graz: 1963) (Kölner Historische Abhandlungen, Bd. 7), *passim*.

they subjected the soldiers under their command. The best-known —but by no means untypical—case was Colonel Schwarz's treatment of the Semenovskii Guard Regiment. His brutality provoked the soldiers of the Emperor's favorite regiment to open mutiny, though a peaceful one, in 1820. Alexander reacted violently: instead of trying to understand the reason for the soldiers' behavior, he punished them with utmost severity, disbanded the regiment, and scattered its officers and men among line units. In so doing he contributed to the spread of dissatisfaction and disaffection in the army.

To enlightened contemporaries the system of military colonies which was energetically promoted after 1815 seemed the crowning stone of Alexander's brutal and senseless militarism. Whatever their potential good and positive features, the military colonies in fact meant additional hardship for all peasants and soldiers involved, a burden for the Treasury, and a new field for exactions and abuse by unscrupulous officials. The Decembrists condemned the system out of hand and poured their passionate hatred on its instigator and executors.[14]

One argument advanced in favor of the military colonies was that they would provide means for improving the condition of state peasants and eventually also set the pace for the progressive emancipation of all serfs. The Decembrists realized, of course, that serfdom was Russia's major social problem. They were well acquainted with its horrors and unanimously agreed that it had to be abolished. But they also were conscious of the difficulties in the path of emancipation and considered that it had to bring about genuine freedom, not a new form of economic bondage, as had been the case of the serfs of the Baltic provinces, who had been freed without land and had remained at the mercy of their former masters. Nor should the nobility be undermined economically. Conscious of this dilemma the Decembrists had no adequate program on serfdom. However, an influential element of the Russian elite had become aware of the serf system's intolerable injustice, as well as of its social danger, and was willing to tackle its abolition in practical terms. The growing number of serf rebellions that punctuated the

[14] R. Pipes, "The Russian Military Colonies 1810-1831," *Journal of Modern History*, XXII, No. 3 (Sept. 1950), 205-19.

reign of Alexander confirmed their diagnosis and underscored the
need for a prompt solution.

The social, economic, and political stagnation of the country,
the preference given to foreigners, the neglect of Russia's true national interests, the "paradomania," and the military colonies were
all the result, the Decembrists were convinced, of the policy and
will of one man, the Autocratic Emperor. Faith in the enlightened
despot, which had characterized eighteenth-century political thought
in Russia as well as in Western Europe, belief that an orderly and
well-organized bureaucracy could bring about the conditions necessary for the happiness and welfare of all subjects, had vanished.
The Russian elite found itself stymied at every twist and turn by
the Autocrat, his whims, and arbitrary decisions. And still worse,
the Autocrat made it possible for the bureaucracy to operate without adequate supervision or controls. An effort had been made to
put the bureaucracy under some restraint by the establishment of
proper rules and channels of communication. But the effort was not
followed through. Its main architect, Speransky, was disgraced and
exiled; the system remained half finished and chaos reigned. After
1815, because of Alexander's frequent absences and lack of interest
in domestic affairs, the Russian government was deprived of whatever unity of purpose and supervision it had possessed. Alexander's
factotum, Count A. A. Arakcheev, the "corporal of Gatchina,"
brought to public affairs the martinet mentality, the prejudices, and
the methods of Paul I's garrison ways.[15] The Decembrists made many
detailed concrete criticisms of the administrative institutions. The
most heavily criticized area was the administration of justice. Quite
rightly the Decembrists considered the judiciary the most corrupt,
inefficient, arbitrary, and confused branch of the government. The
Emperor himself was well aware of the situation and had at various
times tried to remedy it, but without success. Spurred by the criti-

---

[15] Kenneth R. Whiting has tried to "rehabilitate" Arakcheev, pointing out
that he was merely the obedient and ruthless executor of Alexander's will
and that many tales of his brutality are legends. Whatever the truth of
this interpretation, the fact remains that for his contemporaries (as well
as later generations) Arakcheev was the embodiment of all that was hate-
ful in Russia's administration in the last decade of Alexander's reign.
Kenneth R. Whiting, "Aleksei Andreevich Arakcheev" (unpublished Ph.D.
dissertation, Harvard University, 1951).

cisms of the Decembrists, Nicholas eventually did bring some degree of order and equity into the Russian judiciary.[16]

It is now clear that the criticism of the Decembrists was focused on one single basic feature of the Russian situation, the source of all the evil: lack of security and respect for the individual, his dignity, his honor, his property, his work, and even his life. The main cause for this situation was the autocracy and the arbitrariness and whims of its agents. This was naturally the case for the peasant serf; but it was equally true for the townspeople. More important, it was also largely true for the nobility and the educated elite. Russian noblemen had the not unjustified feeling that the Emperor's attitude toward them was quite ambivalent. Alexander I repeatedly expressed his scorn and distrust of the nobility, and so did his closest advisers.[17] No wonder that in turn the nobility was divided in its feelings toward the monarch. In condemning particular abuses, the Decembrists condemned absolutism in general, demanding greater respect for the enlightened and useful members of Russian society (meaning mainly the educated nobility) on the part of the Autocrat and his officials.

It should be added, though, that the Decembrists remained loyal to the monarchy; their loyalty led many to fall into the traps that Nicholas I set them during their interrogation and trial. Paradoxically, many still nurtured the hope that the ruler's goodwill might be used to eliminate abuses and to set firm rules for the conduct of officials; in short they would have liked the monarch voluntarily to set limits on his sovereign power. Even more important than this enduring reliance on the personal character of kingship was the Decembrists' shift of allegiance from the ruler to the "state." It was the first time that an influential group in Russian society held a conception of the Russian state as distinct and separate from ruler, people, and specific administrative institutions. The Decembrists did not advocate a decrease in the authority of the state (in Pestel' 's

---

[16] Mainly by ordering and carrying through the codification of Russian Law, which was accomplished by Speranskii in 1832.

[17] See Grand Duc Nicolas Mikhailovitch, *Le Comte Paul Stroganov, II* (Paris: 1905), and the instances adduced by S. A. Korf, *Dvorianstvo i ego soslovnoe upravlenie za stoletie 1762-1855* (St. Petersburg: 1906), Chaps. 6 and 7.

case they even wanted to increase it immeasurably), as the intelligentsia and revolutionaries were to do later. For the Decembrists the welfare of the people—of the fatherland—were indissolubly tied to the power and dignity of the Russian state.

The contriteness which many Decembrists displayed after their failure was perhaps due to a realization that their enterprise threatened the state as much as the autocracy (Nicholas did not fail to stress this connection whenever possible during the investigation to obtain their confessions). The Decembrists also had come to the conclusion that the prosperity and security of the state did not depend exclusively on the concentration of all sovereignty in a single individual. A good and comprehensive system of institutions, even decentralized along federal lines, could preserve the Empire intact and enable it to resist foreign enemies without resorting to tyranny at home. Paradoxically perhaps, while stressing their commitment to the Russian national state, the Decembrists exemplified the elite's growing alienation from the "government," from the Establishment headed by the Emperor. In this they were only carrying to its ultimate conclusion a trend that had become apparent at the end of the eighteenth century. It is this commitment to the notion of a national state that later generations were to lose completely—ironically, because of the Decembrists' fate. In this respect, as in some others, the Decembrists were not merely a generation of transition, but also the only generation in the history of the modern Russian elite to try to lay the foundations for a meaningful, peculiarly Russian, organic synthesis between the political traditions of the eighteenth century and the historicist and nationalist ideas of the early nineteenth. This is what Speranskii had tried to do in the area of administration by combining the rationalist, mechanistic approach of eighteenth-century statecraft with the historicism of the nineteenth-century nationalists and romantics. Pushkin's poetic work illustrates a similar synthesis of classicism and romanticism—a respect for the state as carrier of the nation's history, combined with an eighteenth-century belief in a rational order securing the happiness and freedom of the individual. The Decembrists combined love of nation and respect of the state, without sacrificing one to the other; their conception of liberty blended the happiness and freedom of the individual with a strong sense of responsibility for the welfare of the group. The balance they had tried to strike was not pre-served by later generations.

Born at the turn of the century, most members of the Decem-brist movement experienced the influence of two different styles of thought and culture. There is no doubt that they were first of all shaped by the world in which they grew to manhood and in which they lived—the first decades of the nineteenth century, the era of Napoleon and its immediate aftermath. None of the Decembrists consciously experienced the French Revolution: their knowledge of it was indirect, but they grew up in its shadow, and its ideas and accomplishments blurred and merged with the traditions of the Enlightenment. But Napoleon's impact was very direct and power-ful. His victories and conquests meant national humiliation and oppression, and, consequently, aroused nationalist fervor and as-pirations. These in turn fostered an interest in and glorification of national history, as well as an emotional commitment to the people and its traditions. Nationalism, of course, was intimately connected with and sustained by romanticism. It permeated all European literature, thought, and life in the early years of the nineteenth cen-tury and it also deeply affected the generation of the Decembrists.

Besides its nationalism, romanticism exalted the creative role of the outstanding individual and stressed society's duty to foster and bring out all potentialities slumbering in him. Inasmuch as the Decembrists felt that Russia's political and social circumstances were the chief barrier to the individual's full development, their ener-gies were channeled into political discussion and action. The ro-mantics proclaimed that the creative individual, the visionary, the leader, isolated from and misunderstood by the vulgar crowd, asserts himself and conquers his freedom through dramatic revolt. The generation of the 1810's had had a taste of the active, heroic, exhilarating life during the wars against the French. The stifling banality and coarseness of the routine imposed by Alexander I after the return of peace bred disillusionment and alienation and pushed the youth, brimming with passion and hope, into rebellion. Noble examples and sources of inspiration were not lacking either. The seething opposition to Metternich's police and the stirrings of national liberation led to the heroic sacrifices of Karl Sand and

Diego Riego and the exhilarating successes of Simón Bolívar and Alexander Ypsilanti.

Romantic exaltation was nourished by literature and in turn it created its own literary movement. Not content with passively experiencing the influence of the German and English romantics, the Decembrists actively participated in the creation of a national Russian romantic literature. Besides counting several significant writers in its own ranks (Ryleev, Bestuzhev-Marlinskii, Kiukhel-beker), the Decembrist movement contributed many members to all the important literary societies of the day. This participation often began in youth and adolescence; as students of Moscow University's Boarding School for Noblemen or the Corps of Cadets, future Decembrists (Turgenev, the Murav'ev brothers) organized or joined literary circles, where they experienced their intellectual and spiritual awakening together.[18] In the latter part of the 1810's K. Ryleev was active in the "Free Society of Lovers of Russian Literature" and through fellow members he came into contact with the Northern Society. Some Decembrists (like A. D. Ulybyshev) were connected with the literary and philosophical group of the Green Lamp in the 1810's, and others with the still more famous literary society, Arzamas, of which Pushkin was the shining light.

ΧA most striking aspect of romanticism was its idealism, in both the epistemological and moral sense. Philosophically, romanticism was based on the idealistic conceptions of the German post-Kantian philosophers, particularly Fichte, Schelling, and Hegel. Perhaps even more important than the writings of these philosophers was their "popularization" through German romantic poetry, drama, and

---

[18] Most important was the "Friendly Literary Society" in Moscow, where N. Turgenev and the Murav'ev brothers made their debut. The Society's rules and meetings have a very strong resemblance to those of the Unions of Salvation and Welfare which N. Turgenev and the Murav'evs helped to organize. See V. M. Istrin, "Druzheskoe literaturnoe obshchestvo," *Zhurnal Ministerstva Narodnogo Prosveshcheniia*, August 1910, pp. 273-307, and March 1913, pp. 1-15. On the connection of this society and the romantic movement in Russian literature, see Marcelle Ehrhard, *V. A. Joukovski et le préromantisme russe* (Paris: 1938). It was these circles also that gave rise to the intense romantic friendships so characteristic of Russian life in the first third of the nineteenth century. See also the recent study by V. Bazanov, *Uchenaia Respublika* (Moscow-Leningrad: 1964).

fiction. The young educated Russians either had read the philosophers' works (for example, N. Turgenev and his circle, many of
whom had studied in Goettingen) or heard of their ideas from
friends and fellow members of the secret societies. The *Tugendbund*,
whose influence on the Unions of Salvation and of Welfare has already been noted, derived its moral inspiration from German idealistic philosophy, especially from Kant and Fichte (the latter's "Letters to the German People" became the call to action for students
and youth). In its social aspect, the idealism of the Decembrists
endowed their desire for change with moral pathos and fervor.
Freedom and beauty, as well as justice, were to be enthroned to
help awaken a stronger sense of social responsibility and humani-
tarian concern for fellow man.

It is one of the paradoxes of the history of Russia, and of its
intelligentsia in particular, that often the knowledge of Russia
stemmed from a preceding discovery of Europe. The young officers
who crossed the borders in pursuit of Napoleon and marched
through all Europe to Paris were better prepared to seek and gain
knowledge of the West than were their fathers and grandfathers
(who also had followed the army into Europe during the Seven
Years' War and the Italian Campaign). Indeed, they had received
a good European education, and they did not merely ape the external forms of Western civilization, as had many eighteenth-century
Russians, but they had a full and true understanding of its spirit as
well. They were familiar not only with European dress, fashions,
arts, drama, but also with its philosophy, serious literature, history,
and intellectual life. In addition, the ideological aspect of the war
against Napoleon, which even the Russian government could not
ignore, had opened their eyes to the political and social events
around them.[19] The hardships that the war brought to their own
fatherland aroused their interest in the conditions of daily life in

---

[19] A printing press and editorial office were attached to Kutuzov's headquarters in 1812-13, which issued propaganda material, addressed to the
peoples of Europe, in which national liberation and political reform were
promised on behalf of the Emperor of Russia and his allies. A. S. Kaisarov,
a friend of the Decembrist N. Turgenev, was one of the chief editors of
this press. See R. E. Al'tshuller and A. G. Tartakovskii, eds., *Listovki
Otechestvennoi voiny 1812—Sbornik dokumentov* (Moscow: 1962).

the West. Finally, contact with fellow officers of the allied armies (especially with the Germans who were fighting for the liberation of their country) called their attention to the social and political institutions of post-Napoleonic Europe. After the war, during the occupation of France they became directly acquainted with political debates, parties, and struggle in a constitutional monarchy by gaining access to influential political and literary salons.[20]

Coming from a country where people were frightened, sullen, and distrustful, the Decembrists were first struck by the free and self-assured behavior of the West Europeans. This impression was particularly strong in Germany after the expulsion of the French, extending even to the lower classes. The soldiers, too, free from the oppressive constraint to which their Russian comrades were subjected, displayed a sense of dignity and independence.[21] The Decembrists quickly discovered the reason for this state of affairs: the rule of law prevailing in the West which gave security to the individual and made arbitrary brutality unnecessary. They noted that such an atmosphere was conducive to a greater concern for man's welfare, material as well as spiritual. Nobody was excluded from this concern, not even the animals, as V. Raevskii observed in connection with a visit to a veterinary school.[22] Little wonder that the West was so much more prosperous; even the peasants of war-torn Prussia and eastern France compared favorably with the poorer nobleman in Russia. Explaining the economic prosperity of the West by the moral and spiritual civilization there, the Decembrists were convinced, in good eighteenth-century fashion, that the basic cause for this favorable state was the high level of enlightenment in Europe. More education, therefore, was the answer for Russia's ills. They eagerly seized upon the opportunities offered by their stay in the West to broaden their own education, attending lectures, con-

---

[20] Even though this was true of only a minority of Decembrists, many more learned about these experiences from participants' accounts.

[21] General Volkonskii wrote, for example: "What most attracted my attention was the absence of rigidity in their [English soldiers'] individual bearing and the ease with which they marched in step." S. G. Volkonskii, *Zapiski* (St. Petersburg: 1902), p. 384.

[22] "[Veterinary school] where through experiments and examples given by enlightened persons, young men were taught to do good even to cattle." Cited in G. Batenkov, I. Pushchin, E. Toll, *Pis'ma* (Moscow: 1936), p. 19.

ferences, and courses. They set up schools of mutual instruction for their soldiers, the so-called Lancaster schools, of which they had seen successful examples in England and Switzerland.[23]

The Decembrists came to Western Europe quite ignorant of their own country, with which they had had little contact in childhood and adolescence, due to the isolation from his own people and country in which the average Russian nobleman grew up and lived in the eighteenth and early nineteenth centuries.[24] Their shock was great when upon their return to Russia they discovered its true condition. Having witnessed the material life in the West, they now saw what the people's circumstances really were: poor, ignorant, oppressed, "backward" in all respects but their spirit and their traditional moral ideals. The immediate effect of this discovery was a revolt against the system. If the more fortunate Russians were worse off than those who were considered deprived in Western Europe, Russia's bad institutions and the evils of its social system were to blame. Such a realization reinforced their discontent and strengthened their will for change. Having learned in war to fight evil, what was more natural than to plan for active combat against the social and political evils at home? The Germans with their *Tugendbund* had shown the way; the writers and political leaders of Western Europe were a source of constant inspiration, as could be learned by reading European newspapers. After 1815 political literature and the study of political science became the most popular pastime. So much so, as a matter of fact, that special lectures or reading and discussion groups were organized with the participation of university professors and members of the Academy.

The Decembrists' discovery of Russia also focused their atten-

---

[23] The Southern Army in the Ukraine later became one of the major areas of application of this new insight. General M. Orlov set up Lancaster schools in his regiments, and Colonel Pestel' took charge of soldier education throughout the Second Army (the schools gave the government its first inkling of the activities of members of secret societies in the army). On the role of formal university attendance by future Decembrists, see M. Wischnitzer, *Die Universität Göttingen und die Entwicklung liberaler Ideen in Russland im ersten Viertel des XIX. Jahrhunderts* (Berlin: 1907).

[24] See M. Raeff, "Home, School, and Service in the Life of the 18th Century Russian Nobleman," *Slavonic and East European Review*, XL, No. 95, June 1962, 295-307.

tion on its people and its past. The Decembrists were perhaps the first among educated Russians to be aware of the individuality of this past, of the particular character of all its periods and its institutions. In their eagerness to revive some of these institutions or to use them in exemplary fashion, the Decembrists still thought in terms of eighteenth-century "pragmatic history." [25] How could it have been otherwise? For their education had been that of eighteenth-century Western Europe and they shared with their older European contemporaries a "philosophic" approach as well as a thorough grounding in classical history and mythology. Because of the time lag between Russian and Western intellectual life, the Decembrists resembled in many ways the generation of Frenchmen that had led the first years of the Revolution. Like them the Decembrists were steeped in the libertarian heroism and drama of ancient Greece and Rome, as it has been painted by Plutarch and Cornelius Nepos. The infatuation with classical antiquity, which had been merely superficial decorative veneer for their fathers, now—under the impact of the French Revolution and Napoleon—assumed vital existential meaning for the Decembrists and became their inspiration and model for action.

But not only in their love for antiquity were the Decembrists children of the eighteenth century. Born in its last decade, they had been raised by parents and educated by teachers who were fully men of the eighteenth century. The Decembrists, therefore, could hardly have failed to absorb its enlightened rationalism, universalism, and faith in progress, albeit in an attenuated form diluted with sentimental, nationalist, and idealistic notions. Rationalism stressed system and implied the belief that progress in human welfare could be achieved on the basis of abstract notions that were to be found in natural reason and deduced from eternal natural laws. This eighteenth-century bent to abstractness and a predisposition toward utopianism are most clearly discernible in the writings of the cool and sober Pestel'.

Freemasonry had been very popular among the Russian nobil-

---

[25] See H. Trevor-Roper, "The Historical Philosophy of the Enlightenment," *Studies on Voltaire and the 18th Century*, Th. Besterman, ed., XXVII (Geneva: 1963), 1667-88.

ity in the eighteenth century. Besides its utopian aspect, it offered an opportunity for displaying the eighteenth-century love for rules, rational hierarchy, and ritualism. But it also stressed the need for knowledge, spiritual progress, and individual perfection for those occupying responsible positions in society. Masonry also emphasized social service and pioneered in undertakings that aimed at spreading education, alleviating misery, and inculcating notions of social solidarity. The Masonic lodges with which Novikov's and Radishchev's followers were associated had called the educated nobleman's attention to the moral wrong of serfdom and impressed on him the necessity of treating the peasant like a person. The fathers of many Decembrists had been associated with Masonic lodges (for example, Murav'ev, Turgenev, Bestuzhev). In some cases, there had been direct contact with leading Masons, like the nephew of Novikov who enlisted Pestel' into the Union of Welfare.

Masonry also emphasized a spiritual approach to religion. It stressed the ethical and mystical elements of individual religious experience as contrasted with the empty ritualism of the official Church. This religious aspect harmonized well with the concern for the life of feeling, spirit, and imagination which characterized romanticism. The sentimental, mystical, and personal religiosity of their fathers affected the Decembrists also. It prepared them to welcome and participate in the religious revival that swept Russia, and Western Europe, during and after the Napoleonic wars. This revival often led to the obscurantism of a Sturdza, Magnitskii, or Krüdener—sponsored by Alexander I and condemned by the Decembrists—but it found expression in such socially progressive and liberal undertakings as the Bible Society, the journalism of Labzin, and the organization of popular schools. The Decembrists were close to these groups, and the constitutions and activities of the secret societies were often patterned after the Masonic lodges to which many members had belonged. Thus the Unions of Salvation and of Welfare and the Order of the Russian Knights imitated some of the ritual and hierarchical organization of Masonry. In short, the Decembrists expressed the political, intellectual, and spiritual seekings of the generation that had been born amidst the whirlwinds that had shaken the *Ancien Régime* everywhere. They were searching for answers not merely in daydreaming and moody introspection, as did the romantics in Germany and England, but in active participation in political struggle. They were willing to do everything necessary to express their ideas and feelings.[26]

It is difficult to speak of an historically significant group whose members were all highly individualized personalities as if it were a homogeneous whole. The Decembrists, even the one hundred twenty odd who received sentences for their role in December, 1825, had as many individual characteristics as they had traits in common. It was not so much their common social class, nor their closeness in age that makes them a definable group. It is rather their sharing of the same historical experiences, mainly the Napoleonic wars.[27]

At first glance we are struck by the large number of their leaders who had served, or were still serving when arrested, in the Guard Regiments. They belonged to the elite regiments, which were stationed in St. Petersburg and whose staff were close to court and government circles. But they were also in the forefront of Russian culture. They had received the best education available, either from private tutors or in select schools for children of the nobility. It was their large-scale participation in the secret societies that impressed and frightened Nicholas particularly. Their arrest and conviction affected practically all of the most prominent families of the realm. It reinforced Nicholas' suspicion of the upper strata of Russian nobility and created a strain between the government and the elite, a rift that fostered the deeper split between society and state and drove the Emperor to harden the bureaucracy's discretionary power.

It would be wrong to generalize, but it should be noted that among the leaders not a few had had rather difficult personal lives or service careers. Not everybody was as much of an outcast and misfit as P. G. Kakhovskii seems to have been. Yet the number of those who, rightly or wrongly, felt mistreated by life is rather high. Many grew up away from their families in the cheerless surroundings of state

---

[26] Leo Tolstoi has given a compelling and accurate picture of this atmosphere of seeking as experienced by Pierre Bezukhov in *War and Peace.* The more difficult circumstances of this search in Russia after 1815 have been dramatized by Griboedov in *Woe from Wit.*

[27] H. Lemberg, *Die Nationale Gedankenwelt,* has coined the apt term of *Generationsgemeinschaft* for it.

boarding schools and corps of cadets.[28] Others experienced disappointments and difficulties in their service careers. But there were also men who, like Turgenev and the Murav'ev brothers, had been surrounded by loving and caring families and whose careers benefited from the influential sponsorship of the best circles of Russian society. Finally, there were the born rebels, in love with their role, arrogant and vain, always pitted against society, but also capable of high-minded generosity and foolhardy courage (M. Lunin, for instance).

Most of the Decembrists were very young. They were adolescents when they joined the secret societies and many were still adolescents at the time of their trial. It is not surprising that the movement itself had a quality of childlike playacting about it, both in the good and bad sense. Good, because they brought youth's generosity, courage, daring, and passionate involvement and idealism to their aims and aspirations. Bad in that they lacked a sense for responsible and orderly action, a notion of the feasible, patience and experience in planning, and balanced and mature estimate of the situation and of their task. The playlike organization and activities of their societies make one wonder at times whether they realized that they were dealing with inflexible human material and body social.

It is in this that the resemblance to their eighteenth-century fathers is most striking. The eighteenth-century nobleman readily acted out in real life what he had learned from Western sources. The serfs (or soldiers) were an easily available and seemingly infinitely plastic material which could be fashioned at will, without regard to their tradition and interests. But what in the eighteenth century had been mere selfish indulgence that took no notion of the serfs' suffering and hardships, became in the early nineteenth century a social concern. The Decembrists did not endeavor to implement reforms to indulge their whims or derive selfish advantage (excluding any unconscious psychological satisfaction, which cannot

---

[28] "In my young days, like yours [his daughter] now, I did not see people and the world. . . . For many years I did not know freedom; I only knew my fellow pupils in my educational prison. . . ." So wrote (in good verses, much superior to this prose rendering) the "first Decembrist," V. Raevskii as he recalled his youth for the benefit of his daughter. P. E. Shchegolev, *Pervyi Dekabrist Vladimir Raevskii* (St. Petersburg: 1905), p. 7.

be documented). They did it in order to serve their country, their nation, and their people. It is true, here too they were following the example set by some of their fathers. In the eighteenth century service had been an ideal and norm which the nobleman flouted at the risk of being considered unworthy of his privileged status. The nobleman's obligation to serve carried with it the leadership of Russian society's progress and westernization. Thus at the end of the eighteenth century we detect a gradual and subtle shift in the object of this service. Since Peter's time the nobleman had served the Emperor and the government, but now—under the influence of Western ideas, of Masonry, and of spiritual religion—he began to think of himself as the servant of the people. The nobleman was increasingly alienated from the government, which did not need him as much any more, and turned to his nation, having at last become conscious of the peasant serf's humanity. Radishchev, whose works and life were well known to most Decembrists, illustrates poignantly and effectively this change in orientation of the best men in Russian society. The Decembrists carried further, with greater passion and exaltation, this particular heritage of the Russian elite's thinking and values.

This heritage may perhaps help to explain the conduct of the Decembrists during their trial and exile. Many broke down easily and repented of their role in Senate Square or in the Ukraine. Besides individual cases of failure of nerve, these breakdowns may be attributed to the effects of a harsh captivity, and the more or less subtle psychological pressures and police tricks for which their background had not prepared them. But such explanations would not be adequate. Many Decembrists were men of great courage and resolution and had entered on the conspiratorial path fully aware of its possible consequences; but many of them felt that their failure to do something valuable and good for their country stemmed from a wrong approach. Then the old concepts of service and loyalty to the state and Emperor again took the upper hand.

None of the Decembrists tried to escape from prison or exile; all accepted their fate with equanimity (at times even too submissively, perhaps). Two reasons probably explain their behavior: First, a sense of shame for their failure and for having followed what was apparently the wrong approach. It was not a sense of guilt for their aims, for they firmly maintained their conviction that their goals had been just; only a feeling of guilt for having failed. They accepted their fate as a deserved punishment for failure and a vindication of their inner righteousness. In the second place, educated Russian society, too, believed that the Decembrists had not done anything basically wrong even though they may have been mistaken about the means. All enlightened Russians understood and shared their purpose and aspirations, for they were in the tradition of service to country and people in which the eighteenth-century elite had been raised. The Decembrists' youth should have been enough to excuse their violent actions; but their judges took no account of it. Society's sympathy for the Decembrists also stemmed to some extent from the latent conflict between nobility and autocracy. The nobility felt slighted by the autocracy, shut out from genuine participation in the formulation of state policy, and they experienced an alienation from the absolute monarchy, which they had helped to create and which now, they believed, had been captured by the bureaucracy. Such an attitude on the part of society provided comfort and material support to the Decembrists in prison and exile; it confirmed their belief that their five comrades who had been hanged were genuine martyrs and that they themselves were carrying on their duty toward their people by serving their unjust sentences. Indeed, their sentences at hard labor, prison, and exile proved that the government considered them a real threat and that their future "martyrdom" justified their actions and redeemed their failure. By living on in chains, exiled in Siberia, they kept alive the flame they had kindled for their people's freedom, for social progress and political reform (and in fact they contributed greatly to the spread of education and welfare in Siberia).

It might be argued that had Nicholas executed all the Decembrists their activities would have been only a relatively unimportant episode in the long and dark history of the Russian autocracy. But by allowing them to live on, making it possible for them to write their memoirs and to be an example of heroic sacrifice for another generation or two, he transformed their failure into victory. The events of December 14 are in truth not the first Russian revolution, as some have labelled it, but the opening episode of *the* Russian revolution. Herzen, the great mythmaker of the Russian revolutionary movement, interpreted and used the Decembrists' fate in this sense. The Russian intelligentsia and the revolutionary leadership followed suit.[29]

The fate of the Decembrists was at the source and the immediate cause of the split between the state and society, the opposition between "we" and "they" proclaimed by Herzen and his generation. The Decembrists performed this historical role precisely because in their own minds there had not been such a split. They had great respect for political authority and they conceived of Russia's transformation in terms of a reform of the *state;* they gave priority to the power and security and welfare of the state. But, in the minds of their families and of succeeding generations, the state which they had wished to improve and which they had loved and defended (from itself, if necessary) had rejected them, cast them out, and martyrized them. What kind of state, what kind of government was it to treat so harshly and unjustly Russia's best men who had nothing but its interest, glory, and welfare at heart? There could be no common language between such a state and educated society. Thus arose a wall between state and society that even the revolution of 1905 could not breach effectively.

Myth and legend are often more significant historically than the real events that gave them birth. Perhaps the Decembrists would have disowned the interpretation of which they became the subject (and some tried to in the 1860's). But precisely because their fate provided the material for a powerful revolutionary legend, they cannot be put in the same category as the Guards who carried out the palace coups of the eighteenth century. There was, no doubt, a superficial similarity between the events of December, 1825, and the many palace coups of the eighteenth century. In both cases the Guards took an active part and in both cases the conspirators tried to put their own favorite candidate on the throne. But behind this apparent similarity there was an ocean of difference. The Decembrists had discussed ideological questions and had tried to formulate constitutional programs and reforms. None of the Guard groups that carried out the coups in the eighteenth century had done so. The Decembrists were motivated not only by selfish

---

[29] Lenin's sanction (with some minor qualifications) of this interpretation is the justification for the energetic and vast amount of study done on the Decembrist movement in the Soviet Union.

interests. True, some of their proposals, if implemented, would have benefited primarily themselves and the nobility; but they would also have benefited the rest of the country and would have initiated a long series of far-reaching transformations. The Decembrists were sincerely and honestly concerned with improving the lot of their fellow Russians. The Guard leaders of the eighteenth century had nothing but selfish aims in mind; they craved only material and service advantages as reward for their revolt; they were utterly alien to the idealistic and moral passion that animated the Decembrists.

It was their sincerity and passion that made the life of the Decembrists an example to be emulated, and that inspired their myth and legend. To equate December 14, 1825, with 1741, 1762, or 1801 is to forget—what Pushkin with his unerring insight was quick to note—the historically creative role played by the Decembrists' style of life and death. This role made the Decembrist movement one of the most significant events in nineteenth-century Russian history and thought; it justified the Decembrists' being called the fathers and first martyrs of the Russian Revolution.

II

Critique of Conditions and Fermentation of Minds

The secret societies that eventually led to the formation of the Northern and Southern Societies of the Decembrist movement arose in response to two sets of forces: (1) criticism of the conditions prevailing in Russia; (2) general intellectual and spiritual malaise and an urge to help Russia join Europe on the road to even greater happiness and progress.

1. The conditions prevailing in Russia after the end of the Napoleonic wars helped to highlight the basic economic and social ills of the Russian polity. The great cost of the wars had resulted in a severe economic crisis, and the hardships and mismanagements provoked by the conflict underscored the basic injustices of the social and political system. The young educated Russians who had fought in the wars and seen its liberating effects on Western Europe were of course disappointed that no extensive reforms were introduced in Russia, which needed them much more than Western Europe. Their experiences in war and abroad had cemented close emotional bonds. Common interests and readings led to a desire to act together. Together, therefore, they discovered the main causes for Russia's ills, which fell into two general categories: The basic aspects of the system (consisting mainly in the structure of Russian society), and the overly centralized, arbitrary administration. The specific

problems lay in certain institutions, serfdom, the economic consequences of the wars, the recruitment of officials, and the poorly conceived procedural innovations in several areas of the administration.

After their arrest, the Decembrists talked little of the general features of the Russian polity; most of them even were at pains to stress their loyalty to the Sovereign. But they talked rather freely and at length on various specific evils they had noted. The Chief Secretary of the Investigating Commission, A. D. Borovkov, kept the minutes of the interrogations and also carefully read and reviewed their written testimonies. On the basis of this information he compiled a rough digest of the main points of criticism made by the Decembrists. This Digest was later turned over to the Commission of the 26th of December, 1826, set up to make proposals for reform on the basis of the testimony.

As the Decembrists themselves were not always clear or explicit, and as they did not always focus on specific and essential things, their testimonies resulted in listing particular grievances and criticisms, rather than offering a comprehensive general evaluation of the situation. In accurately reflecting this feature of the testimonies, the Digest itself suffers from some incoherence, unevenness, and allusiveness.

2. The spiritual malaise and intellectual ferment that took hold of Russia's young generation who reached maturity during the Napoleonic wars is best reflected in the answers the Decembrists gave to specific questions put to them by the Investigating Commission. The question as to the source of their revolutionary or rebellious (or merely discontented) frame of mind elicited answers that allow us to reconstruct quite accurately the intellectual physiognomy of the Decembrists. Of course these were replies made by accused prisoners to their judges. Not all Decembrists could preserve equanimity of mind and spirit under the conditions of their arrest and the psychological pressure to which they were subjected. Some tried to exculpate themselves, many more endeavored to play down their radicalism, and a few even attempted to shift the blame onto others and onto external circumstances. The selections from the testimonies given below try to illustrate most of these attitudes, and also to present the various experiences through which the Decembrists arrived at their "liberal" ideas and revolutionary activities. We see how the eighteenth-century patterns of thought and action were gradually displaced by those of the nineteenth; but in the minds of

most Decembrists they continued to coexist harmoniously to a surprising extent.

*Digest of the Testimony Concerning the Internal
Conditions of the State Given by the Members of the
Subversive Society* by A. D. Borovkov
From Iu. G. Oksman, ed., *Dekabristy—otryvki iz istochnikov*
(Moscow and Leningrad: 1926), pp. 2-9.
(Originally in *Russkaia Starina*, 1898, No. 11, pp. 353-62.)

1. Introduction

The most brilliant hopes for the prosperity of Russia marked
the beginning of the reign of Emperor Alexander I. The nobility
relaxed; the merchants did not complain about credit; the military
served without hardship; scholars studied whatever they wished;
everybody could say what they thought; and from the great good of
the present everybody expected better things [to come] still. Unfor-
tunately, circumstances did not allow this to happen, and the hopes
grew old, unfulfilled. The unlucky war of 1807 and other costly campaigns ruined finances. Napoleon invaded Russia and it was then
that the Russian people perceived their power, it was then that the
feeling for independence—first political, later also national—was
kindled in every heart. This was the origin of the ideas of liberty in
Russia.[1] The government itself pronounced the words: liberty, liberation. Itself it disseminated works on the abuses of Napoleon's unlimited power. The war was still in progress when the returning
soldiers' grumblings first spread among the people: "We have spilled
our blood," they said, "but they force us to sweat again at corvée;
we have freed the country from the tyrant, but our lords tyrannize us
again." Having returned to the fatherland, the armies—from general
down to soldier—continuously spoke of how good it was in foreign
lands. At first, as these talks went unhindered, they were cast in the
wind, for the mind, like gunpowder, is dangerous only when com-
pressed. Many were warmed by the efforts of some generals to free

---

[1] In all our sources, the Russian terms *svobodomyslie, vol'nodumstvo, vol'nyi
obraz myslei* are used. Although their original meaning was "free-thinking"
—in the eighteenth-century, Voltarian (anticlerical) sense—in the context
of the Decembrist movement and uprising they took on the connotation
of ideas of freedom, liberty, and, more loosely, of liberalism.

their serfs and by the hope that the Sovereign Emperor would give a constitution, as he had mentioned at the opening of the Warsaw Diet.[2] But everything changed from 1817 on: men who noticed the evils and who wished the good were forced to speak in secret for fear of the many spies, and this circumstance brought them closer together.

2. Education

The true roots of republican enthusiasm were hidden in the very education and upbringing which for twenty-four years the government itself had given the young. It was the government which, so to speak, had nursed their liberalism; on entering life, at every step, [the youth] came upon a reason for reaching the goal to which such an education leads.

3. Laws

Firm, clear, and concise laws, etching themselves easily into the mind, prevent abuses. With us one decree is piled on top of another: the one destroys and the other renovates; for every case there are found many mutually contradictory acts. As a result, the mighty and the slanderous triumph, while the poor and the innocent suffer.

4. Justice

The very organization of our judicial system is extremely complicated. From the Land Courts (*zemskii sud*) to the Council of State there are so many steps that much time and great means are required to carry a lawsuit through all instances in which decisions are rendered and overturned; and frequently the decisions rendered by the highest jurisdiction merely enable the litigation to be started anew in accordance with [proper] procedure. Thus, a lifetime is not enough to await the end [of a litigation]. Add to this the injustices, abuses, and bribes that completely ruin the litigants.

---

[2] In the speech from the throne in 1818, at the opening of the Diet that had been established under the constitution granted to the kingdom of Poland in 1815, Alexander I made vague allusion to his hope of eventually granting Russia proper an order of government similar to that enjoyed by Poland. His ambiguous and vague words were interpreted by most Russians as a definite promise of a constitutional monarchy.

5. System of Administration

Inconstancy characterized the government, and no positive and firm plan was followed in administering the State.

A. *Statute on the Provinces*[3]

The Statute on the Provinces had been changed in its basic principles; the power of the lower courts had been weakened; the governors had appropriated all local power; the establishment of governor-generals had completed the destruction of provincial institutions; all affairs had been concentrated in their [governor-generals'] hands; even the government saw everything only through their eyes. Yet for twenty-five years nothing in particular had been done to improve the administration of the provinces. In 1822 Governor-General Balashev was authorized to make an experiment in reform.[4] Begun without the Senate's knowledge, the experiment was greeted with indignation by the population because of the new burdens and increase in official institutions; and no one spoke of the good that ought to come from it.

B. *Colleges*

The Colleges which Russia owed to Peter the Great, and which over the course of seven reigns had stood firm amidst many internal changes, were abolished.[5]

---

[3] The Statute on the Provinces, 1775, had attempted to extend the area of autonomous administrative action on the local level by providing for the participation of lower police and court officials elected by local assemblies of the nobility.

[4] General Aleksandr Dmitrievich Balashev (1770-1837) had been Minister of the Police and of the Interior. He proposed to combine several provinces under a Lieutenant of the Emperor to bring about greater decentralization in the administrative structure of the Empire. The plan was briefly tried out in only one case; several provinces near St. Petersburg were combined under the administration of Balashev himself.

[5] The Colleges (*kollegiia*), established in the reign of Peter the Great, had been the highest executive departments. They were organized along functional lines and on a collegiate principle (headed by a board whose president was only *primus inter pares*) and gave way to Ministries organized along monocratic lines (the minister was complete master in his ministry) in 1802.

C. Senate

The Senate, this depository of the laws and guardian of public order, had been transformed into a mere printing press, subjected to every favorite's [whim].

D. Ministries

The creation of Ministries, replete with serious fundamental defects, had obviously been carried out in haste. The Ministries were handicapped by not being adequately connected with the provincial administration.

E. Committee of Ministers

The Emperor's absences from the capital provided the pretext for establishing the Committee of Ministers.[6] Nothing better could be invented to hide all the disorders from the Sovereign and to show only a façade to the people. All business was transacted in secret; under the guise of simplicity and speed, procedural forms covered up all negligence and arbitrariness. The Chancelleries [of the Ministers] could do anything they wished, and instead of [having] the individual responsibility that had been promised when the Ministries were established, everybody—including the Ministers—was covered by His Majesty's authorizations and the Sovereign had to bear alone the brunt of all mistakes and disorders.

This led to three important consequences: (i) Numerous minor affairs, taken up to the Committee, were forwarded to the Sovereign, needlessly burdening him. (ii) Every official in the Ministry could easily hide his mistakes and secure private benefits without fear of being brought to account. (iii) Imperial orders lost their natural force and importance.

But this was not all: new ways of confusion were discovered. Because of the large number of particular affairs, various [Ministerial] Committees were established with the same authority as the main Committee. One committee would decide all over again

---

[6] A very common source of antigovernment criticism were Alexander I's frequent absences from the capital (as in A. Pushkin's poem "Skazki—Noel," 1818).

business [transacted by] another. [Several] decisions pertaining to the same question and confirmed by the Sovereign Power [i.e., Emperor] were often in complete contradiction one to another. Thus, in the last years, the central government disintegrated, so to speak, lost its unity, and became a huge, shapeless thing.

6. Decline of Civil Affairs

Civil affairs in general—the keystone of the State's welfare—were to some extent in disfavor. The late Emperor saw the evils, considered them to be incurable, and limited himself to showing his disgust, because he could think of no one who could help him to undertake reforms.

7. Salaries of Officials

The salary of an official should ensure his livelihood. With us it is completely out of balance. The civil governor, master of a whole province, is allotted less than a vice-governor, and all the officials in charge of an entire district together receive less than one liquor-tax inspector. How many officials, with barely anything to do, receive huge salaries from two or three offices, how many of these also receive pensions? But an incomparably larger number lives in poverty, even in want of their bare subsistence.

8. Conditions of the Clerks

The condition of the clerks is worthy of pity: for thirty or forty paper rubles[7] a year they are fated to work from morning to evening. One need only to see the wretched condition of these people in the provinces to take pity on them.

9. Collection of Taxes

Taxes collected for the citizens' benefit will not be burdensome, especially if they are assessed on the interest from capital and do not

---

[7] Russia was on the silver standard at the time; but since the reign of Catherine II the government had also printed paper rubles, so-called assignats. As the circulation of paper increased (to cover the heavy military expenditures in the first decades of the century), the value of the paper ruble dropped; after 1815 it hovered around 25 per cent of the value of silver.

destroy the latter. But what a wide scope for abuses and popular misery was provided by [the existence of] local dues, arbitrarily imposed by local authorities! There was no check and no accounting procedures were observed in increasing taxes, especially personal dues. The people could not fail to feel their burden. A governor needed only to wish a reward, and an entire province had to make the greatest sacrifices.

10. Road-Maintenance Duty

It is enough to point out the incessant sending of peasants to road-construction duty, frequently at the peak of the busy season, during hay gathering or harvest time. This obligation has ruined villagers completely; in part, because of the frequent changes in [work] plans, and in part because of the abuses by local (*zemskii*) officials who first build and then tear up under pretext of poor workmanship, or who assign those who live near to faraway jobs and vice versa, so as to receive money for exemptions.

11. Arrears

The people, burdened by wrongful tax collections and various work obligations, have fallen into arrears. The very strict measures taken to collect the arrears have completed their ruin. Peasants began selling cattle, horses, and their very houses, while in some provinces the expressions "beat out," "knock out" arrears have become technical terms. One should add also that almost all of the capital and its circulation have been centralized in the capital city situated in the [far-off] corner of the Empire. That is where most treasury offices are located and where the most important work is performed. For this reason the remote provinces, and those away from waterways connecting with the capital, have deteriorated and experience want in everything.

12. Government Enterprises

The Treasury has aspired to monopoly. Under pretext of economic considerations, the government has gradually become separated from the people and deprived entire families of their subsistence by taking from them the activities they have engaged in since time immemorial. Instead of being spread among the people, various improvements were made the exclusive property of the Treasury, which naturally was beyond competition from private individuals.

A. Sale of Liquor by the Treasury

The system of the sale of liquor, because of its wide impact, is one of the most disastrous features of the Treasury's monopoly. It has completely ruined many noble families whose situation had already been shaken by the mortgaging of almost all their estates to the "twenty-four-year bank." [8] It has been a temptation to officials, for . . . enrichment was preferred to honor. It has changed large sums into idle capital, as the officials who had enriched themselves most frequently either did not dare or know how to make good use of these fortunes. It has served as the source of an exceedingly harmful popular vice. Everywhere there has been an increase in taverns and other drinking establishments, some with billiards, music, and other popular attractions. In the first years, such a policy indeed brought revenue, but it turned out to be temporary; during recent years far fewer millions have been collected.

B. Treasury Sale of Salt

The price has been increased on salt, one of the main necessities of life. Before 1812, so as to lighten the burden of the poorest classes of the population, the government not only derived no revenue from it, but even suffered losses.

C. Collection from Tax Farmers and Government Contractors

In recent years the Ministries have acted terribly. Tax farmers and contractors were subjected to strict and unfailing recoveries; but when they made claims against the Treasury, they were left to shift for themselves. Doing business with the Treasury ruined the

---

[8] In the eighteenth century the nobles had distilled alcohol on their estates and sold it to cities and faraway provinces. "Twenty-four-year bank" is a reference to liberal credit terms granted by government banks to the nobility, especially to help repair the damage wrought by the invasion of 1812.

most prominent merchants and contractors, as well as the latter's creditors, because of delayed payments, discounts, and unjust exactions and deliveries.

D. Violation of the Good [Principles] of Management

. . . Nowhere was genuine management practiced. Management consisted merely of artificial accounts which were not balanced against the accounts of previous years or against those of the other institutions directly concerned.

13. Trade

The Tariff of 1810, which had been beneficial to Russian industry, was in 1816 suddenly replaced by a twelve-year tariff in favor of Austria, Prussia, and Poland. At any rate, businessmen [felt they] could make deals on the basis of this fixed period. But they were wrong: there followed in 1819 a new general permission to import foreign goods, which soon flooded Russia. Many merchants went bankrupt, manufacturers were completely ruined, and the people were deprived of their livelihood and of means to pay taxes. Then the error was noticed and corrected by the Tariff of 1823. But the harm could not be undone. The inconstancy of tariffs not only ruined industrialists, but undermined trust in the government. Finally, in 1824, an additional act pertaining to the guilds was issued and followed up by many additions and explanations; but with all this the local authorities could not put into effect [this legislation], for the poor townspeople, especially those in small towns, had been deprived of all means of subsistence. In this manner our trade sickened.

14. Condition of the Navy

On the basis of the Admiralty Regulation of Peter the Great, every shop had to be given its assigned share of work as soon as a ship's keel was laid, so that all things necessary for outfitting her be ready at the set time. But during the entire administration of the Marquis de Traversay[9] this [rule] was not followed. Ships were built

---

[9] Prèvost de Sausac, Marquis de Traversay (1754-1830): Minister of the Navy 1811-28.

every year, they were brought to Cronstadt, and then they frequently rotted there without making a single voyage. This is how the last forests are being destroyed and money spent. But there is no fleet.

15. Military Colonies[10]

A. Settlement

The compulsory settlement was greeted with astonishment and murmurs. Then the colonies' goal was made public: to free Russia from the burdensome obligation of furnishing recruits. But lowering the length of service to eight or twelve years would have accomplished this purpose more equitably, simply, and less dangerously, for the military spirit would have been disseminated throughout all of Russia and peasants would have parted from their children as easily as do the noblemen: Upon returning to his family [the recruit] would be able to marry and follow the peasant's calling and . . . he would bring up his children to be soldiers later, while remaining himself in readiness for the militia.

B. Economic Aspect

Military settlements are supposed to be economical, partly because they are given favored treatment by the Commissary and [Army] Supply services. In fact this is not so: they cost much in money, land, forests, labor, and people. If one makes a correct calculation, the revenue, at 5 per cent interest, on the capital needed for . . . settling some regiment of the First Grenadier Division would assure the complete maintenance of this regiment forever.

---

[10] A policy was introduced by Alexander I under which regiments were settled on the land and their soldiers forced to combine agriculture with military duties. State peasants were transferred to these colonies and compelled to undergo military drill and exercises, as well as cultivate the land. Based on Byzantine and Austrian examples, in the mind of Alexander I the military colonies were to introduce a system of militia armies and pave the way for a reform of serfdom. In practice, however, the establishment of the colonies brought even greater hardship on the peasantry. The system was universally hated and provoked peasant rebellions which were drowned in blood. See Richard E. Pipes, "The Russian Military Colonies 1810-1831," *Journal of Modern History*, XXII, No. 3, (Sept. 1950), 205-19.

16. Classes of Citizens

A. *Noblemen, Landowners*

The conduct of noblemen with respect to their peasants is horrible. To sell [members of] families separately, to rape and debauch peasant women, not to speak of the burdens of corvées and quitrents, is considered to be nothing at all and is done openly. In particular, the small landowners are Russia's cancer: . . . they always grumble, and as they wish to live according to their caprices and not according to their means, they mercilessly torment their poor peasants.

B. *Personal Noblemen*

Personal nobles without estates, like the Polish *szlachta,* multiply rapidly. They consider any work and craft to be lowly and they live by various dodges; in general they are the type of men who expect to gain something from change and who can lose nothing.

C. *Clergy*

The village clergy is in a wretched state. Without any salary, they are entirely at the mercy of the peasants whom they have to please; but from this they fall into vice to such an extent that by decree the government, through the civil governor, had to forbid the parishioners from making the priests drunk. While the village clergy remains in poverty and ignorance, the decree on the clothing of the priests' wives stirred the discontent of the rich urban clergy.[11]

D. *Merchants*

The merchants, hampered by guilds and difficulties of transportation, have suffered great losses since 1812. Many capitalists perished, others were ruined. . . . The number of fraudulent bankruptcies increased and confidence fell. The privilege which ennobles citizens belongs [now] to wealth and not to persons. This has two consequences: [(1) For example] a rich honest merchant is ruined

---

[11] Apparently there was some legislation against excessive display and luxurious apparel of the wealthy city clergy.

through no fault of his; the loss of capital is in itself a misfortune. But instead of consolation, the law brings further misery by depriving him of those very rights that distinguished him from the lower classes. [(2)] The virtuous but poor merchant remains in a lower status, while the dishonest, but rich one, having declared his capital, obtains rights that make him the equal of the most distinguished nobility. Here is temptation that destroys civic virtue.[12]

E. Townspeople (meshchanin)

The class of townspeople is important and esteemed in other countries, but in Russia it is insignificant, poor, crushed by dues and taxes, and deprived of the means of [earning a] livelihood; the latter, in particular, [is the consequence] of the regulation which provides that if they wish to engage in retail trade [townspeople] must either enroll in a guild or obtain affidavits with payment of dues. Because of their poverty, they have been particularly affected by the decline in trade.

F. State Peasants

Dependent on the Land and District Courts, the provincial administration, and the Chamber of the Treasury, the state peasants are completely ruined by the frequent raids of officials from these institutions. Everybody subjects them to exactions, everybody makes demands on them; but nobody cares for them or is responsible for their welfare. The Chamber of the Treasury has, it is true, an economic section that manages state lands, but its influence is weak, for the Land Police, District Court, and provincial administration have equal or even greater influence.

G. Appanage Peasants[18]

The appanage peasants are cited in contrast to state peasants and their condition is described [as being] in the best [of] conditions.

---

[12] Merchants who declared a large capital were often granted personal noble status. They lost this status when their wealth declined below a certain point.

[18] Peasants on estates belonging to members of the Imperial family.

They enjoy rights, have their [own] office [*kontora*] not only to administer them, but to defend them against oppression by the Land Police and other authorities. The manager of the office is responsible for the administration of the peasants under his jurisdiction. But his powers are limited: he cannot arbitrarily impose his fancies or, without special permission of the Minister, dismiss the village head elected by the community. The apportionment of all taxes and the issuance of regulations are decided by common counsel.

17. Conclusion

The brief description of the condition of the country shows under what difficult circumstances the presently reigning Emperor has assumed the scepter and what great obstacles lie across his path in overcoming the difficulties: give laws, insure justice by establishing a speedy judiciary administration, raise the level of the clergy's moral education, strengthen the nobility that has declined and has been utterly ruined by the "twenty-four-year law," resuscitate trade and industry through permanent statutes, give youth another type of education appropriate to all conditions, improve the situation of the husbandman, destroy the degrading sale of men, resurrect the navy, encourage individual persons to [take up] seafaring and to follow the appeals of Haiti and America—in short, correct the innumerable disorders and abuses.

Minister of War, TATISHCHEV
State Councilor, BOROVKOV

[The preceding Digest was read and discussed by the so-called Committee of the 6th of December, 1825, set up to examine the needs of Russia in the light of the evidence given by the Decembrists. The following entry in the minutes of the Committee describes its members' reaction to the reading of the Digest: Minute No. 29, meeting of 27 March 1827.]

From "Bumagi Komiteta
6 dekabria 1825,"
*Sbornik imperatorskogo
russkogo istoricheskogo obshchestva*,
74 (St. Petersburg: 1891), 94.

Thereupon was read the Digest, compiled in the Ministry of War, of the testimonies of members of the subversive society concerning the condition of the State. [The Digest] contains many truths to which the government has in part already paid attention; but the existing evils are highly exaggerated, which was to be expected of people who wanted to cover their design with an acceptable pretext. However that may be, the Committee has decided to make all possible use of this information in its future work.

Excerpts from Individual Testimonies

The Investigating Commission demanded from every prisoner written answers to a standard questionnaire. Three questions from it elicited answers best revealing the Decembrists' intellectual development and frame of mind.

Question 4

Where have you been brought up? If in a public institution, which one specifically, and if at the home of parents or relatives, who were your teachers and tutors?

Question 6

Have you audited special lectures in addition [to regular schooling]? In what fields, when, with whom, and specifically where? Indicate the textbooks you have used in studying these disciplines.

Question 7

When and from where did you acquire liberal ideas? From contacts with others or from their suggestion, from the reading of books or works in manuscript? Specifically which ones? Who helped to reinforce these ideas [in you]?

Prince Sergei Petrovich Trubetskoi[14]
From *Vosstanie Dekabristov,* I (1925), 8-9.

Answer to Question 4

I was brought up in the house of my father; my governor, from infancy to the age of sixteen, was an Englishman named Izinevud [Easonwood?]; my teachers were: for German, pastor Lundberg; for French, an émigré, captain in the royal French service, Stadler. The latter lived in my father's house for four or five years. My teachers in Russian and mathematics came from the gymnasium of Nizhnii Novgorod. When I was seventeen years old my father took me to Moscow, where I attended some lectures at the University, while a teacher of mathematics and fortifications came to our house.

Answer to Question 6

I audited a special course of lectures on the Statistics of Russia and on political economy by Professor German,[15] I believe in the winter of 1816-17, but perhaps I am mistaken about the year. . . . In Paris, out of curiosity, I heard almost all the famous professors several times, except for the professors of natural science whose courses of lectures I heard in full. I was guided in my studies . . . by the best-recognized textbooks in these fields.

Answer to Question 7

I acquired liberal ideas at the end of the war against the French, as a result of the events that had occurred after the establishment of peace in Europe, such as: the transformation of the French Empire into a constitutional monarchy; the promise of other European sovereigns to give their peoples a constitution, and the latter's introduction into several countries; the annexation of the kingdom of Poland and the establishment there of a government

---

[14] Sergei Petrovich Trubetskoi (1790-1860): Colonel with General Staff of the 4th Infantry Corps; one of the directors of the Northern Society, slated to become dictator in case of the revolt's success.

[15] Carl Theodor Hermann, in Russia Karl Fedorovich German (1767-1838): statistician and political economist; member of the Russian Academy of Sciences.

of this nature; the first speech of the late Emperor at the Diet of Warsaw, from which it was inferred that His Majesty intended to lead Russia, in due course, to a similar state; in this [last] opinion we were confirmed by: (1) the freeing of the peasants in the German provinces,[16] and we believed that this measure would be extended to the Russian and Polish provinces; (2) the return of its rights to the former province of Finland. Discussions I heard in society concerning these matters, conversations with members of the former secret societies, the reading of journals and of books dealing with the history and legislation of various countries, contributed to this [liberal] way of thinking. In it I was confirmed in my conviction that Russia's condition was such that an upheaval would unavoidably occur in due time; I based this opinion on: (1) the frequent rebellions of the peasants against their landlords, the increases in number and length of these rebellions; (2) the universal complaints of extortions by officials in the provinces; and finally (3) on [the belief that] the establishment of military colonies would in time also become a cause of upheaval.

Kondratii Fedorovich Ryleev[17]
From *Vosstanie Dekabristov*, I (1925), 156.

Answer to Question 7

I was first infected by liberal ideas during the campaign in France, 1814-15. Then [my liberalism] gradually grew from reading various contemporary writers, such as Bignon, Benjamin Constant, and others;[18] my criminal cast of mind was set from the day I be-

---

[16] The serfs in the Baltic provinces had been freed, without land, in 1816 and 1819.

[17] Kondratii Fedorovich Ryleev (1795-1826): executive secretary in the offices of the Russo-American Company, formerly a Freemason, had been one of the most active members of the Northern Society; also the most prominent poet among the Decembrists.

[18] Louis Pierre Edouard Bignon (1771-1841): French diplomat and author of many influential books on contemporary politics and history. Benjamin Constant (1767-1830): prominent French journalist and writer; a member of the group of liberal "idéologues" in the first years of Napoleon's regime, he became one of the most prominent spokesmen for liberalism during the Restoration.

came a member of the society and for a period of three years [had] almost daily conversations with people of the same frame of mind and continued reading the authors mentioned. No one in particular has reinforced these ideas in me and for all I must blame myself alone.

Prince Evgenii Petrovich Obolenskii[19]
From *Vosstanie Dekabristov,* I (1925), 226.

Answers to Questions 4 and 6

I was educated at my parents' home. My tutors . . . were French governors who changed every year and sometimes even twice a year and left no trace of their teaching, so that I can hardly remember the names of two or three of them: Chevalier d'Ayanger, Comte Tilly; the others I can't recall, since there were sixteen or eighteen of them.

Upon entering service, and especially after my promotion to officer, I noticed the inadequacy of my knowledge in political science, which had become the subject of general conversation after the return of the Guard in 1814; I therefore began to study contemporary and ancient history, political economy, and law. In 1819 I attended Professor Kunitsyn's lectures on political economy,[20] but I truly don't recall where. As far as I recall, Professor Kunitsyn relied on the textbooks of Storch and Say.[21]

Answer to Question 7

I acquired a liberal way of thinking from the time I entered service—through intercourse with educated people who had par-

---

[19] Prince Evgenii Petrovich Obolenskii (1796-1865): Adjutant in the infantry Guard Regiment; member of the Union of Welfare and of the Northern Society.

[21] Heinrich Storch, in Russia Andrei Karlovich Shtorkh (1766-1835): Vice-President of the Academy of Sciences. Jean-Baptiste Say (1767-1832): French political economist.

[20] Aleksandr Petrovich Kunitsyn (1783-1840): jurist; exponent of Natural Law at the University of St. Petersburg and other institutions of higher learning.

ticipated in the campaign of 1812; through the reading of various books on politics; through reflection and membership in a society that had political goals. This way of thinking was strengthened by the spirit of the age and by observation of the events which during the last years had punctuated with all kinds of revolutions the history of almost all countries of the world (except Africa). In truth, I cannot say what specific books have influenced my way of thinking, for my readings have been quite varied. In general, my way of thinking was furthered by the reading of publicists like Benjamin Constant, Bignon, etc. I do not recollect having read any particular works in manuscript. No one has reinforced me in my thinking, which was entirely the result of the above cited causes.

Nikita Mikhailovich Murav'ev[22]
From *Vosstanie Dekabristov,* I (1925), 294.

Answer to Question 7

The proclamations of the Allied powers in 1813, offering the peoples of Germany a representative government as a reward for their efforts, called my attention to this question for the first time. In this I was later confirmed by the late Emperor's speech to the Diet of the kingdom of Poland, in which he announced his intention to introduce representative government in Russia. I did not read any manuscripts. Neither books nor persons have influenced me.

Petr Grigor'evich Kakhovskii[23]
From *Vosstanie Dekabristov,* I (1925), 343.

---

[22] Nikita Mikhailovich Murav'ev (1796-1843): Captain of the General Staff of the Guards; founder of the Union of Welfare; one of the directors of the Northern Society and author of its Constitutional Project.

[23] Petr Grigor'evich Kakhovskii (1797-1826): Lieutenant, retired; graduate of the Moscow Boarding House for the Nobility; active member of the Northern Society; shot and killed General Miloradovich on December 14, 1825, as the latter was trying to talk the soldiers massed on Senate Square into returning to their barracks.

Answer to Question 7

Ideas are formed with age. I cannot specifically say when my notions were developed. Studying the history of the Greeks and Romans from childhood, I was fired by the heroes of antiquity. The recent revolutions in the political organization of Europe affected me deeply. Finally, the reading of everything known in the field of politics gave my ideas direction. In 1823 and 1824 I was abroad, I had many occasions to read and to study—isolation, observation, and books were my teachers.

Alexsandr Aleksandrovich Bestuzhev-Marlinskii[24]
From *Vosstanie Dekabristov,* I (1925), 430.

Answer to Question 7

I acquired my liberal ideas mainly from books; moving gradually from one opinion to the other, I became so engrossed in the writings of French and English publicists that the speeches in the Chamber of Deputies and in the House of Commons fascinated me as much as [they would] a Frenchman or Englishman. Among the modern historians the greatest influence was Heeren and among the publicists, Bentham.[25] Concerning Russian works in manuscript, they were too unimportant and slight to make an impression; I read none of them, except "On the necessity of [permanent] laws" by the late Fonvizin, two letters of Mikhail Orlov to Buturlin, a few poetic sparkles by Pushkin.[26] I do not wish to accuse anyone of implanting this way of thinking. I was searching for such contacts myself. More-

---

[24] Aleksandr Aleksandrovich Bestuzhev-Marlinskii (1797-1837): Staff Captain in the Dragoons; active in various periodical journals; member of the Northern Society; turned himself in and confessed on the night of December 15, 1825; well-known author of short stories based on his observations and experiences after 1826 in the army in the South.

[25] Arnold Hermann Louis Heeren, (1760-1842): German historian; author of the popular *Handbuch der Geschichte des Europäischen Staatensystems und seinen Colonien.* Jeremy Bentham (1748-1832): English philosopher; founder of Utilitarianism.

[26] Denis Ivanovich Fonvizin (1745-92): Russian playwright; his treatise on the desirability of fundamental laws for the Russian Empire was written in 1783 and circulated in manuscript form in the high circles of St. Petersburg society. Mikhail Fedorovich Orlov (1788-1842): Major General; had been close to the Decembrists and was a member of the Union of Welfare, but did not actively participate in the events of 1825.

over, I will say, not in my defense though, that hardly less than one-third of the nobility thought the way we did, albeit they were more cautious.

Mikhail Aleksandrovich Bestuzhev[27]
From *Vosstanie Dekabristov,* I (1925), 481-82.

Answer to Question 7

In 1817 I graduated from the [Naval Cadet] Corps and in the same year I was sent to France with the fleet under the command of Vice Admiral Crown. There I made the acquaintance of many French officers and English travelers and acquired the principles of liberal ideas. Returning to Arkhangel'sk in 1824, we stopped in Copenhagen where I had occasion to become acquainted with Danish and English naval officers. The ideas I acquired in France were strengthened in their company. In addition, since our own fleet had been in England in 1812 and since our naval officers yearly visited England, France, and other foreign countries with our navy, they had acquired a notion of the systems of government there. Their descriptions, which I had occasion to hear involuntarily, nourished the notions I had already acquired. The revolutions which had occurred almost everywhere in Europe and about which one could obtain adequate information in Russian newspapers were cause enough for the strengthening of the ideas and notions I had received.

Otherwise no one contributed to strengthening these ideas in me.

Aleksandr Nikolaevich Murav'ev[28]
From *Vosstanie Dekabristov,* III (1927), 8.

Answer to Question 7

I acquired my insane liberal ideas during my stay in foreign countries from the spirit of the age, that is, during and after the

---

[27] Mikhail Aleksandrovich Bestuzhev (1800-1871): Staff Captain, brother of Aleksandr Bestuzhev-Marlinskii; member of the Northern Society.
[28] Aleksandr Nikolaevich Murav'ev (1792-1861): Colonel of the General Staff of the Guards, retired; member of the Union of Welfare.

War of 1813-14. This lead me to read various books on politics, such as Machiavelli, Montesquieu, the *Contrat Social* of J. J. Rousseau, etc. I have read no manuscripts. All these books and many others, written not under the guidance of God's True Light which only illuminates the souls of his true worshippers, but under the influence of man's own damaged reason, devoid of the light of faith, have sown in my heart and mind the harmful seeds of their errors and fancies which, until 1819, kept me under their nefarious influence. But the Commission already knows how in May, 1819, through the grace of God and His great pity, I was converted, I confessed, and solemnly and openly renounced the criminal society, and how the Lord saved me from the deep and dangerous abyss over which I was standing. . . . During the last seven years not only did I not participate in the society, but tried to convince others to leave it.

Ivan Dmitrievich Iakushkin[29]
From *Vosstanie Dekabristov*, III (1927), 44.

Answer to Question 7

I cannot recall that any particular person or the reading of some [particular] books exclusively aroused liberal ideas in me.

My stay abroad during the military campaigns probably drew my attention, for the first time, to the social organization of Russia and compelled me to see its defects. After my return from abroad, serfdom seemed to me the only obstacle to the drawing together of all classes and . . . to the civil reorganization of Russia. Residing for a time in the provinces and frequently observing the relations between serfs and landowners, I was more and more confirmed in my opinion.

In my first testimony I indicated how I became one of the first to agree to the organization of a secret society. I cannot say that anyone's acquaintance or persuasion forced me to forget all my obligations and surrender to a stupid and criminal indignation against the government; it was rather the doings of my youth, my

---

[29] Ivan Dmitrievich Iakushkin (1796-1857): Captain, retired; member of the Union of Salvation and of the Union of Welfare; member of the Northern Society; arrested in Moscow.

unbridled personality, my passions, and the feeling of an excess of vitality.

Mikhail Sergeevich Lunin[30]
From *Vosstanie Dekabristov*, III (1927), 128.

Answer to Question 7

A liberal cast of thought took shape in me from the moment I began to think; natural reason strengthened it.

Mikhail Fotievich Mit'kov[31]
From *Vosstanie Dekabristov*, III (1927), 192.

Answer to Question 6

I did not attend special lectures. But during my stay in Paris in 1824 and 1825 I listened to some lectures but did not take a course. I heard lectures on French rhetoric by Mr. Villemain, on phrenology by Gal [sic], on philosophy by Dunoyer, on history by Arto and Villemain, on chemistry and physics I do not remember by whom.

Answer to Question 7

I acquired the nefarious liberal ideas which led me into such horrible errors from reading books and from the company of Nikolai Turgenev, who more than anyone was instrumental in imparting such ideas.[32]

---

[30] Mikhail Sergeevich Lunin (1787-1845): Lieutenant Colonel of the Hussars; resided in France, 1816-17, where he converted to Catholicism; aide-de-camp of Grand Duke Constantine in Warsaw; member of the Southern Society.

[31] Mikhail Fotievich Mit'kov (1791-1849): Colonel; member of Masonic lodges and of the Northern Society.

[32] Nikolai Ivanovich Turgenev (1789-1871): high official in the Council of State and the Ministry of Finance; member of the Union of Welfare; abroad during the events of 1825, he became an émigré; wrote the well-known book, *La Russie et les Russes* (Paris: 1847), one of the first comprehensive accounts of the development of Russian political ideas and public opinion.

Pavel Ivanovich Pestel' [33]
From *Vosstanie Dekabristov*, IV (1927), 89-92.

Answer to Question 4

Until the age of twelve I was brought up in my parents' home. In 1805 I went with my brother (who is now Colonel in the Regiment of Cavalier Guards) to Hamburg and from there to Dresden, from where I returned in 1809 to my parents' house. During our absence from the fatherland, our education was guided by a man called Seidel, who, after entering Russian service, was on the staff of General Miloradovich in 1820. In 1810 I was admitted to the Corps of Pages, graduating in 1811 as lieutenant of the Lithuanian Life Guard Regiment. . . . I had not the slightest conception of political sciences until I began preparing for entrance into the Corps of Pages, where this subject is required for admission to the upper grade. I then studied it under Professor and Member of the Academy German, who at the time was teaching the subject in the Corps of Pages.

Answer to Question 7

I cannot name any person whom I would credit with imparting the first free thinking and liberal ideas or the exact time when they began to take shape in me. For this did not happen suddenly, but imperceptibly. . . . When I had acquired a pretty solid notion of political sciences I became passionately interested in them. I was glowingly enthusiastic and with all my heart I wished for good. I saw that both the happiness and misery of states and nations depended to a large measure on the government, and this conviction gave me [still] greater inclination toward those sciences that deal with such questions and point to the means [for solving them]. But at first I studied these sciences and read political books in all humility, without free thought, with only the one wish of being in due time and in my position a useful servant of Monarch and Country. . . . I also paid attention and gave thought to the condition of the [Russian] people, and here the slavery of the peasants always affected me deeply, and so did the advantages of the aristocracy; the latter I saw as a wall standing between the Monarch

---

[33] See introduction to Chapter V.

and the People, hiding from the Monarch the true condition of the people for the sake of selfish advantages. . . . The return of the Bourbons to the French throne and my reflection on the consequences of this event marked an epoch in my political opinions, my conceptions, and my ways of thinking. For I began to reason that most of the fundamental institutions introduced by the revolution had been maintained at the time of the Restoration of the monarchy and had been acknowledged to be good things, while everybody, including myself, had been against the revolution. This judgment gave rise to the idea that, seemingly, a revolution is not as bad a thing as they say and that it may even be quite useful; this judgment was confirmed by the observation that the states which had not experienced a revolution continued to be deprived of such advantages and institutions [as had France]. . . . In this manner, constitutional as well as revolutionary ideas began to take shape in me at the same time. . . . I was led from a monarchical constitutional way of thinking to a republican mainly by the following facts and considerations: The works of Destutt de Tracy in French made a great impression on me. . . .[34] All newspapers and books praised so much the increase of happiness in the United States of America, ascribing it to their political system, that I took it to be clear proof of the superiority of the republican form of government. Novikov[35] told me of his republican constitution for Russia; at the time I still argued in favor of a monarchy, but later I recalled his judgments and began to agree with them. I recalled the happy period of Greece when it consisted of republics and its miserable conditions later. I compared the great destiny of Rome in the days of the republic with its lamentable fate under the Emperors. The history of Great Novgorod also strengthened in me republican ideas. I believed that in France and England the constitutions served only as covers and did not prevent the English Cabinet and the French King from doing what they wanted. And in this respect I preferred autocracy to such a constitution, for I reasoned that in an autocratic government the unlimited power is openly seen by all; in constitutional

---

[34] Antoine Louis Claude Destutt de Tracy (1754-1836): philosopher; his ideas based on sensualism provided an ideological foundation for French liberalism; wrote *Eléments d'idéologie*, 4 vols., 1817-18.

[35] Mikhail Nikolaevich Novikov (1777-1822): member of the Union of Liberation and of several Masonic lodges; had served in the Chancellery of the Ukrainian governor-general, Prince N. G. Repnin.

monarchies, on the other hand, there also exists limitless power, though it acts more slowly, and because of this it cannot correct evil fast. . . . It seemed to me that the main trend of this century consists in the struggle between the popular masses and aristocracies of all kinds, whether of wealth or of birth. I estimated that, as in England, these aristocracies would eventually become stronger than the monarch himself and that they were the main obstacle to the state's happiness and could be eliminated only through a republican form of government. The events in Naples, Spain, Portugal influenced me greatly then. In them I found irrefutable proof of the lack of stability of constitutional monarchies, and completely adequate reasons for distrusting the sincerity of the monarchs who accepted a constitution. These last considerations strengthened me very much in my republican and revolutionary ways of thinking. . . .

Petr Ivanovich Borisov[36]
From *Vosstanie Dekabristov,* V (1926), 22.

Answer to Question 7

Nobody imparted in me free thoughts and liberal ideas. The reading, since childhood, of Greek and Roman history and of the lives of great men by Plutarch and Cornelius Nepos implanted in me a love for freedom and popular sovereignty. Subsequently, the cruelty displayed by commanding officers toward their subordinates nourished this love and fanned it every hour. In 1819, not long before the Georgian campaign, the commander of my company sentenced [men] to flogging for drunkenness and embezzlement. . . , I was so moved [by the sight of the execution] that I left ranks and swore to myself to abolish this kind of punishment, should it cost my life. The injustice, violence, and oppression of the landlords toward their peasants always stimulated in me similar feelings and strengthened liberal ideas in my mind. To this there were added personal grievances and discontent. . . . The desire to be useful to humanity always filled me, I took as a rule always to seek truth and I thought that I would find it in the opinions that were to be mine. *The general good is the highest law*—on this maxim my religion and my ethics were based. . . .

---

[36] Petr Ivanovich Borisov (1800-1854): Sublieutenant of artillery; co-founder and member of the Society of United Slavs.

Mikhail Matveevich Spiridov[37]
From *Vosstanie Dekabristov*, V (1926), 117-18.

Answer to Question 7

I served mainly in the army and was billeted in the houses of peasants; I confess: examining in detail their condition, seeing how their masters treated them, I was often horrified, felt guilty, and found the cause of it all in their belonging [to landowners]. In the Ukraine I saw in the same village state peasants having everything in plenty, while the lord's peasants suffered poverty. When I was transferred into the province of Zhitomir, I became still more distressed by the general poverty of the peasants. There I saw that a fertile province pays tribute only to landowners; I saw the unceasing activity of the peasant whose fruits served to enrich the lords; I saw the latter's immeasurable wealth in grain, while at the end of the year the peasants lacked not only grain for sale but even for their own sustenance. . . . I confess, my heart was gripped with pity for them. . . . Also outraged by the procrastinating and poor administration of justice, the cruelty toward the soldiers. . . .

Mikhail Pavlovich Bestuzhev-Riumin[38]
From *Vosstanie Dekabristov*, IX (1950), 49.

Answer to Question 7

I drew my first liberal ideas from the tragedies of Voltaire, which to my misfortune fell too early into my hands. Preparing later for the examination provided by the Decree of 1809,[39] I thoroughly studied natural law, civil and Roman law, political economy (all these were required subjects). These studies gave me a love of politics. I began to read well-known publicists, among

---

[37] Mikhail Matveevich Spiridov (1796-1854): Major; member of the Society of United Slavs.

[38] Mikhail Pavlovich Bestuzhev-Riumin (1803-26): Sublieutenant of the infantry; prominent member of the Southern Society and architect of its fusion with the Society of United Slavs.

[39] Legislation requiring the passing of an examination, or the completion of a course of studies, before promotion to a rank equivalent to that of staff officer in the government service (Decree of 6 August 1809, PSZ, No. 23771, the work of M. M. Speranskii).

whom the empty-worded Pradt did the greatest harm.[40] At the same time everywhere I heard the verses of Pushkin which were read with enthusiasm. All of this more and more strengthened my liberal opinions. In view of my career, I concentrated on military books. But I transferred to the army. . . . Here I was invited to join the Society. I had the foolishness to accept. Everything else was the unavoidable consequence of this ruinous first step. . . .

Matvei Ivanovich Murav'ev-Apostol [41]
From *Vosstanie Dekabristov*, IX (1950), 216-17.

Answer to Question 4

When my father was minister in Madrid he did not have the means of educating me at home. My late mother and I traveled to Paris where I lived seven years, attending a public institution (École secondaire de M. Hix). There I managed only to pass the first course in the humanities. I studied mostly Latin and Greek. I had religious instruction from the Embassy's priest. In 1809 I returned to Russia.

Answer to Question 7

The first notions of free thought and liberalism I acquired during our stay in Paris in 1814. Until that time I did not know of the existence of a constitution. I did not even know the term, as I had not studied political sciences. . . . I was animated by love for the fatherland which we had saved from Napoleon's yoke. The reading of foreign newspapers, particularly *Le Constitutionnel,* strengthened these [ideas]. Talking always about the same things, I was led to criminal ideas by the influence of other people. . . . I was destroyed by the wicked influence of the Society. . . .

---

[40] Dominique Dufour de Pradt (1759-1837): French clergyman, diplomat, and publicist; wrote on the South American colonies and contemporary diplomacy.

[41] Matvei Ivanovich Murav'ev-Apostol (1793-1886): Lieutenant Colonel, retired; one of the founders of the Union of Salvation and of the Union of Welfare, member of the Southern Society; participated in the mutiny at Chernigov.

III

Hopes and First Steps Toward Organization

———◆———

To a generation reared in the ideas of the eighteenth century, whose fathers had frequently dabbled in Freemasonry and experienced the revivals of religious commitment and social consciousness in the reign of Catherine II, the discovery of Russia's harsh reality must have come as a shock. And so it did. Brought up to hope for an active role in the service of their country and people (and having had a taste of it during the wars against Napoleon), the young elite found itself stymied by the social and political system and the resulting demoralizing atmosphere.

To this situation the educated Russian could respond first by dreaming about a better future. Such dreaming had been popular in the eighteenth century, when many "utopias" had reflected the hopes and expectations of the would-be reformers. Aleksandr Dmitrievich Ulybyshev follows this tradition in his "A Dream." Born in 1794, he had been educated in Germany; he returned to Russia at the age of sixteen to enter government service (first in the Ministry of Finance, then in that of Foreign Affairs). He was widely read and well educated, and quite prominent in the literary circles and journals of his time. His special interest was music, and he is still remembered for two outstanding studies on Mozart and Beethoven. For his involvement in the Decembrist movement he received only a light sentence, and he died in 1858 in Nizhnii Novgorod, where he had retired at the end of his exile.

Many members of the educated elite had occasion to become directly acquainted with what was taking place in Western Europe in the last years of Napoleon's rule. Particularly, they witnessed the efforts of German youth to bring about the moral and political renaissance of their fatherland by organizing associations and societies. They were especially impressed by the principles and activities of the *Tugendbund* (Society for Virtue), whose members were dedicated to a moral regeneration of their society in preparation for its political liberalization. Nikolai Ivanovich Turgenev (born 1789) had been attached to the staff of the Allied Political Commission, whose head and guiding spirit, Freiherr vom Stein, was entrusted with the administration of the German territories liberated from the French. Turgenev was thus in a good position to become acquainted not only with the ideas of vom Stein—the great reformer of modern Prussia—but also with the *Tugendbund* itself. Upon his return to Russia (where he occupied a prominent position in the Ministry of Finance) Turgenev tried to organize a society of public-spirited men on the model of the *Tugendbund*. His somewhat shapeless and vague first proposal is reproduced here. Nikolai Turgenev himself withdrew from active participation in the Decembrist movement in the early 1820's. As he was abroad at the time of the revolt, he judged it prudent not to return to Russia. He remained in exile and died near Paris in 1871.

The example of the German *Tugendbund* and the efforts of men like Nikolai Turgenev bore fruit in the foundation of several secret societies in the years after 1815. Among these, the Union of Salvation lasted for about a year (1816-17) and was the immediate predecessor of the most important pre-Decembrist society, the Union of Welfare (1818). Practically all the members of the Union of Welfare eventually participated in the Decembrist organizations. It was, however, essentially a society for the dissemination of moral principles and the coordination of socially useful activities within the framework of the existing order. Its Constitution, therefore, contains almost no political elements and, taking the existing order for granted, does not touch on concrete administrative problems. It owes its inspiration to the constitution of the German *Tugendbund,* some of whose organizational rules it follows quite closely.

Indirectly it was influenced by the societies dedicated to the spread of enlightenment and virtue which had been popular in the eighteenth century, specifically, Benjamin Franklin's proposed "Junto" in Philadelphia.[1]

A Dream by Aleksandr Dmitrievich Ulybyshev
From *Izbrannye proizvedeniia Dekabristov*, pp. 286-92.

Of all forms of superstition, the most forgivable, it seems to me, is the interpretation of dreams. Indeed, there is something mystical in dreams that forces us to recognize in their fantastic visions warnings from Heaven or previews of our future. No sooner has the ambitious man surrendered to the sleep which had eluded him for a long time, than he already sees himself decorated with the medal that had been the cause of his insomnia; and upon waking he convinces himself that the Easter feast or the New Year will bring the fulfillment of his dream. In his dreams the unlucky lover delights in the object of his longing, and hope—almost dead— revives in his heart. Oh fortunate ability to feed on illusions! You counteract the real misfortunes with which our life is constantly surrounded; but not only selfish passions are supported by your spells—the patriot, the friend of reason, and especially the philanthropist, also have their fancies which sometimes are embodied in their dreams and give them a minute of imaginary happiness that is a thousand times greater than what sad reality can offer them. Such was my dream last night; it harmonizes to such an extent with the desires and dreams of my friends of the "Green Lamp"[2] that I cannot forbear sharing it with them.

---

[1] On the *Tugendbund* see: Johannes Voigt, *Geschichte des sogenannten Tugend-bundes oder des sittlich-wissenschaftlichen Vereins* (Berlin: 1850); and Paul Stettiner, *Der Tugendbund* (Königsberg in Prussia: 1904).

The plan for a society by Benjamin Franklin: "Standing Queries for the Junto" and "Proposals and Queries to Be Asked the Junto." *The Papers of Benjamin Franklin*, Vol. I, Leonard W. Labarée, ed. (New Haven: Yale University Press, 1959), pp. 255-64. Also under the title: "Rules for a Club Established for Mutual Improvement" in *The Works of Benjamin Franklin in 12 Vols.*, Vol. I, John Bigelow, ed. (New York and London: G. P. Putnam's Sons, 1904), pp. 331-40.

[2] The "Green Lamp" was a literary society closely connected with the Union of Welfare. It lasted from 1818 to 1820.

It seemed to me that I was in the streets of St. Petersburg, but everything had been changed so much that I had difficulty in recognizing them. At every step new public buildings attracted my glance, while the old ones seemed to be used for purposes most oddly different from those for which they had been originally designed. On the façade of "Michael's Castle" [3] I read in big golden letters: "Palace of the State Assembly." All kinds of public schools, academies, and libraries had taken the place of the innumerable [military] barracks which used to crowd the city. Passing before the Anichkov Palace[4] I saw through large glass windows a great number of marble and bronze statues. I was told that this was the Russian Pantheon, that is, a collection of statues and busts of men who have distinguished themselves by their talents and services to their country. I looked in vain for the present owner of the palace.[5]

As I found myself on the Nevskii Proespekt I glanced straight into the distance and instead of the monastery that stands at the [avenue's] end,[6] I saw a triumphal arch which seemed to have been erected on the ruins of fanaticism. Suddenly my ear was struck by sounds whose harmony and unknown power seemed like a combination of the organ, the harmonica, and the serpent—a wind instrument. Soon I saw a huge crowd converge to where these sounds came from. I joined the crowd and soon found myself in front of a rotunda whose size and magnificence surpassed not only all our contemporary buildings, but also the huge monuments of Rome's greatness, whose fragments alone are to be seen now. Bronze doors of extraordinary size stood open to admit the crowd; I entered along with the others.

Inside, a noble simplicity corresponded to the magnificence outside. The interior of the cupola, supported by three rows of columns, represented the Heavens with their constellations. In the middle of the hall rose a white marble altar on which an eternal flame was burning. The profound silence that reigned among the

---

[3] Michael's Castle had been built by Paul I as his residence. It was a semi-fortified palace, which did not prevent Paul I from being murdered there.

[4] One of the imperial palaces in St. Petersburg.

[5] Alexander I.

[6] The Smol'nyi Monastery—at the time it housed also the restricted boarding school for noble girls. (In 1917 it was the headquarters of the Petrograd Soviet.)

assembly, the concentrated looks on all faces, led me to surmise that I was in a temple—but I could not guess of what religion. Not a single statue or image, not a priest whose vestments or gestures could have dissipated my doubts or given direction to my guesses. After a minute of preliminary silence a few extraordinarily just and good voices began to sing the Hymn to Creation. For the first time I felt that the performance was worthy of Haydn's genius, and indeed I thought I was hearing a choir of angels. No doubt, therefore, there also must have been female voices in the chorus, and this innovation, consonant with good taste and reason, gave me an inexpressible pleasure.[7] "If," I reasoned, "the insect with its humming and the bird with its twitter praise the Almighty, what a ridiculous and barbarous injustice prohibits the most interesting half of the human race to sing His praise?" The wonderful sounds of this music, together with the vapors of perfumes burning on the altar, rose in the huge cupola and seemed to take with them the pious thoughts and transports of gratitude and love pouring out to the Deity from all hearts. At last the singing stopped. An old man, decorated with insignias unknown to me, mounted the steps of the altar and spoke the following words: "Citizens, in offering a tribute of gratitude to the Dispenser of all good we have fulfilled a sacred duty; but this duty will be empty form if we do not also glorify the Deity by our deeds. Only if we live by the laws of humaneness and of compassion for our unfortunate brethren can we hope to attain eternal bliss at the price of a few years of virtue." Having spoken this the old man commended to the charity of those present several wretches whose undeserved ruin had been caused by unlucky circumstances. Everyone hastened to help according to his ability, and in a few minutes I saw a sum of money adequate to free ten families from want.

I was astounded by all I saw, and through an inconsistency that is inexplicable but occurs frequently in dreams, I suddenly had forgotten my own name, my country, and felt like a foreigner who has arrived in St. Petersburg for the first time. Approaching the old man I freely entered into conversation with him in spite of his high office. "Sir," I said, "forgive the curiosity of a stranger who, not knowing whether he should believe his eyes, makes bold

---

[7] Women were banned from the choirs of the Russian Church.

to ask you the explanation for so many wondrous things. Do not your compatriots belong to the Graeco-Catholic faith? But the impressive meeting which I just witnessed does not resemble either the Greek or the Latin mass and does not even show traces of Christianity." "Where do you come from then?" replied the old man. "Or has the study of history engulfed you to such an extent that it has resurrected the past, while the present has disappeared from your view? It is three centuries since the true religion has been established among us, that is, the cult of the only and almighty God, founded on the dogma of the soul's immortality, of punishment and reward after death, and purified of all human and superstitious elements. It is not to wheat bread, to the mistletoe on the oak, or to the holy myrrh that we address our prayers, but only to Him whom the greatest poet of a nation that has been our teacher has long ago defined in a verse: 'His name is Eternity and the world His creation.' Among the common people some old women and bigots regret the old rites. Nothing can be more splendid, they say, than to see a mass celebrated by a bishop with a dozen priests and deacons transformed into valets, busily vesting him, genuflecting, and kissing his hand every minute; he sits, while all faithful stand. Tell me, is that not real idolatry, less splendid than the Greeks' but sillier still, because the ministers of God are identified with an idol? Today we have no priests and *a fortiori* no monks. Every high official in turn carries the duty that I fulfilled today. After leaving the temple I shall be busy with judicial matters. Is not the guardian of order on this earth the most deserving representative of God, source of order in the Universe? Nothing is simpler than our rites. In our temple you see neither statues nor pictures; we do not believe that the material representation of the Deity is insulting, but only that it is simply ludicrous. Music is the only art which rightfully is admitted to our temples. It is the natural language between man and God, for it compels one to feel what no words can express and what even imagination cannot create. My duty calls me elsewhere," the old man remarked. "If you wish to accompany me, I shall gladly tell you of the changes and reforms that have taken place in the last three hundred years of which you seem to be poorly informed." I gratefully accepted his offer and we left the temple.

Walking through the city I was struck by the clothes of the inhabitants. They combined European decorum with Asiatic majesty, and upon closer examination I recognized the Russian kaftan with some modifications. "I believe," I said to my guide, "that Peter the Great had ordered the upper class of Russian society to wear German garb. Since when have you given it up?" "Since we have become a nation," he answered. "Since we ceased being slaves we have no longer worn the master's livery. Despite his extraordinary talents, Peter the Great possessed a genius for imitation rather than for creation. By forcing a barbarous people to take on foreign dress and customs he gave them the appearance of civilization in a short time. But this premature civilization was as far removed from genuine civilization as the ephemeral hothouse plant is from the ancient oak that for many years has matured under the sun, in the open, a barrier against storms and a monument to eternity. Peter was too much enamored of his own glory to be completely a patriot. He wanted to enjoy in his own lifetime what could only be the fruit of centuries. Only time creates the great men in all fields who determine the character of a nation and point the path it must follow. The impetus given by that ruler had for a long time held back our genuine accomplishments of civilization. In the fine arts our works, copied from foreign models, preserved for two centuries . . . that difference which separates men from the ape. Our literary efforts in particular carried the seeds of decline before they had reached maturity; and like our institutions, our literature could be compared to a fruit, green on one side and rotten on the other. Fortunately, we noticed our error. Great events, in breaking our fetters, put us in the forefront of European nations and revived the almost dead spark of our national genius. We discovered the fertile and almost untouched vein of our ancient popular literature and from it there soon surged the poetic flame which still burns brightly in our epics and tragedies. Acquiring ever more the traits that distinguish free peoples, our customs gave birth to comedy, native comedy. Our presses no longer are busy increasing and reproducing an unnecessary quantity of translations of French plays, obsolete even among the people for whom they had been written. Following the example of the writers in all the countries that have created their own literature, therefore, it was only by removing ourselves from the foreigners that we could become their equals; and having gained victory over them by our arms, we became their allies in genius."

"Excuse me if I interrupt you, Sir, but I do not see the many military for which you told me your city is the main center."

"Nonetheless," he answered, "we have more soldiers than there have ever been in Russia, for their number reaches fifty million people."

"An army of fifty million men—you are joking, Sir!"

"Nothing could be more correct, for nature and nation are one and the same. Every citizen becomes a hero when he has to defend the land that nourishes him, the laws that protect him, the children whom he raises in the spirit of freedom and honor, and the fatherland whose son he is proud to be. Indeed, we no longer maintain innumerable mobs of idlers and thieves organized into regiments, a scourge not only for those against whom they are sent, but also for the people who feed them; for if they do not destroy entire generations by their weapons, they corrode them at the core by spreading infectious diseases. We do not need them anymore. The scaffolding upholding despotism has come down with it. The people's love and confidence, and particularly the laws that deprive the ruler of the opportunity of abusing his power, surround him with a more loyal guard than 60,000 bayonets. Incidentally, tell me, did the ancient republics such as Sparta, Athens, and Rome, which made themselves illustrious through their warlike feats, did they have permanent armies? The [military] service necessary for the country's internal peace is performed, in turn, by all citizens throughout the Empire who are able to bear arms. You will understand that this change in the military system produced a great change in finances too. Three-quarters of our revenue, previously swallowed up exclusively in maintaining the army (and which did not prevent the latter from dying of hunger), are now used to increase the general welfare, to promote agriculture, trade, industry, and support the poor, whose number, thank Heaven, decreases every year under Russia's paternal government."

At this moment we found ourselves in the middle of the Palace Square.[8] Above the walls of the palace, blackened with age, waved an old flag; but instead of the two-headed eagle with lightning in its claws, I saw on it a phoenix soaring in the sky and holding in its beak a wreath of olive branches and immortelles.

---

[8] Square in front of the Winter Palace, surrounded by government buildings.

"As you see, we have changed the Empire's coat of arms," my companion said. "The two heads of the eagle denoting despotism and superstition have been cut off and from their blood rose the phoenix of freedom and true faith."

Coming to the banks of the Neva, in front of the palace, I saw a splendid bridge, half marble, half granite, leading to a beautiful building on the other side of the river on whose façade I read, "Temple of Justice, open to every citizen, [where] at any hour he can demand the protection of the law."

"In there," the old man told me, "meets the Supreme Tribunal, consisting of the eldest of the nation, to whose number I have the honor of belonging."

I was about to cross the bridge when I was suddenly awakened by sounds of trumpets and drums and the cries of a drunken *muzhik* dragged to the police. I thought that the fulfillment of my dream was still far off. . . .

Ideas on the Organization of a Society
by Nikolai Ivanovich Turgenev
From E. I. Tarasov, ed., *Arkhiv brat'ev Turgenevykh,*
Part V: *Dnevnik i pis'ma Nikolaia Ivanovicha Turgeneva za
1816-1824 gg* (Tom III) (Petrograd: 1921), pp. 368-72.

Many right-minded persons, even those who have the opportunity, feel that there are no ways through which they could call the public's attention to some sound ideas, impart a few correct notions, present some good rules with a beneficial effect. A person who is unconsciously driven to reflect on the welfare, honor, and glory of the fatherland frequently has ideas which he would like to make known; but at the first step he is stopped by various difficulties. The idea disappears in unfulfilled desire.

In recent times there has been a noticeable yearning for general enlightenment; not the kind that is acquired in schools, but the kind that enables a person to evaluate the political [*grazhdanskii*] condition of his fatherland. But how inadequate are our means for acquiring this . . . political enlightenment!

Where can a Russian obtain the necessary general rules of civil society? To this day our literature has been almost entirely limited to poetry. Works of prose do not deal with political sub-

jects. This characteristic trait of Russian literature makes it un-
satisfactory for our times. We now want other moral nourishment,
more substantial, better related to the demands and conditions of
the century. Poetry, and in general belles lettres, cannot fill our
souls, souls open to important and decisive impressions. Lacking
any of our own, we follow the political events in Europe. From
the end of the last century these events have taken on an aspect
that was powerful and majestic, frightening at times, but always
interesting. Nowadays not just an exclusive few are concerned with
the history of contemporary events: everyone, without exception,
wants to know them, judge them. In Russia, too, this aspiration
has been noticed. The human mind always needed nourishment;
[the latter] varied with the spirit of the times. Previously (namely,
in the period of Catherine II) we looked for nourishment in Freemasonry, mysticism, alchemy. Now, when as a result of big events,
the mind of the nations has given up the barren field of gloomy
rêverie and has turned toward earnest reality, now when the spirit
of the times has flown over several centuries in a few years, the
moral requirements of our compatriots have acquired another
character. The Russians, too, want to participate in the destinies of
enlightened Europe; they want to know not only of its prosperity
and miseries, but also of their causes. In this respect the last war
had a decisive impact on Russia. Peter the Great forced us to
march together with Europe. We have followed the direction [he
gave us]; we have marched along an open path, but we did not
know where to and we had no goal. The events of 1812, 1814, 1815
have brought us closer to Europe. We—at least many of us—have
seen the aims of national life, the purpose of the states' existence;
and no human force can make us turn back. The events of the last
thirty years had the important result of illuminating Europe with
genuine enlightenment. Today every European who attentively
reads the newspapers is more enlightened politically than the most
learned men of the seventeenth and previous centuries. Let us here
define the meaning or essence of genuine enlightenment: it consists
in the knowledge of one's rights and obligations. After many errors,
Europe can at last enjoy the fruits of its long existence.

In view of this state of Europe and of Russia, and of the
latter's relationship to the former, one cannot but agree that the
joining together of several Russians who love their fatherland, its

glory and happiness, and who are true to their obligations and to the laws of honor, may be of some use to Russia, provided their active, selfless striving toward a noble goal is crowned with some success. Everything selfless, just, and true must, at the very least, have some measure of success. The single notion of truth cannot be lost, and sooner or later it must produce its effects.

Those who wish to serve the fatherland in this new field of selfless labor are invited to form a society. This society will not be known before the coming together of several members who have become convinced that the society is possible and [who have] means of existence. When it is decided to organize [the society], the members will in due form petition the government for permission to establish the society and secure the government's approval. In the meantime, the members will draft the rules of action for the society, etc. For the present it is proposed that the society have as its aim the *publication of a journal*. This journal will have three sections: I. The first will contain observations and discussions concerning the geography, ethnography, statistics, and history of the Russian state, as well as Russia's legislation and national economy. The supplement to the first part will contain dissertations on the same topics, either written in Russian or translated from foreign languages. II. The second part will contain reviews of books, both Russian and foreign, related to the various disciplines taught in Russian schools and universities. III. The third part will be devoted to literature. It will contain various works, sometimes translations, and also poetry. In addition, there will be a last section under the title of "Miscellany."

By joining the society, active members obligate themselves to submit articles for the journal from time to time. In addition, the society will make efforts to enlist the participation of outsiders in its work. At present, many ideas, many studies concerning Russia remain unknown because their authors do not know, so to say, what to do with them. The society will endeavor to attract the attention of right-minded persons who might be inclined to contribute to its success and, consequently, to the success of a good cause.

Only a few ideas and observations concerning the needs for a society and its goals have been presented here. Those who are accustomed to think about the welfare of the fatherland will find in their own hearts the strongest incentive to organize such a society and to complement with their own feelings this inadequate and inaccurate exposé. (We need not criticism, but enlightenment.) Such men will more readily understand the simple impulse of pure devotion than they will a comprehensive disquisition on a subject that lies close to the heart of the virtuous and of the right-minded.

To date, the idea of the proposed society has been accepted by N. Turgenev and Professor A. P. Kunitsyn.

Constitution of the Union of Welfare
From *Izbrannye proizvedeniia Dekabristov,* pp. 237-76.

"For unto whomsoever much is given, of him shall be much required; and to whom men have committed much, of him they will ask more."
[Luke 12:48]

Introduction

¶1. In nature all physical creatures are governed by manifest laws and these laws define their mutual interaction. Observation shows that the laws are immutable, and everything that appears to be a violation of this order is but their necessary effect with respect to nature. Chance does not befit the Maker, and creation, therefore, has a goal to which tend all laws of nature; the first goal we see is the *general preservation of the creatures.*

¶2. Moral creatures are subject to this goal too, for as every man strives for his own preservation and good, when [several] men combine into society *preservation of the common good* becomes the first law.

¶3. Thus the Maker's first visible goal in creating physical and moral creatures is their common preservation and good; and there is in nature an immutable common goal, so there must be an *immutable [principle of] justice* consisting in the harmony between nature's particular goal and the aim of the Maker. And, furthermore, as nothing can exist in nature separate from nature, no particular goal can be a just one if it does not harmonize with the aim of the common good.

¶4. Not having a will of their own, physical creatures cannot violate the laws prescribed by the Maker; therefore, all their actions are just. Moral creatures, however, combining into societies and manifesting their will through their actions, often violate the happiness of others in a constant striving for their own good. Therefore, it is necessary that they have laws, i.e., conditions directing their mutual actions toward the preservation of both the particular and general good, as well as a government seeing to the execution and improvement of these laws.

¶5. These governments and laws may vary, but each one of them, whatever it may be (if it is just) has and must have as its aim the *good of the ruled.* The Apostle Paul speaks on this subject as follows: "For rulers are not a terror to good works, but to the evil. Wilt thou then not be afraid of power? Do that which is good and thou shalt have praise of the same; for he is the minister of God to thee for good. But if thou do that which is evil, be afraid; for he beareth not the sword in vain; for he is the minister of God, a revenger to execute wrath upon him that doeth evil." [Rom. 13:3-4.] No sooner has the government as its goal the good of the ruled than all the laws tending to this goal become just and their implementation is called *justice.*

¶6. The mutual actions of men, however, are so varied that the laws cannot define all their relationships and for this reason every society leaves still a great deal to the [individual] will of each: to direct these wills toward the government's aim, i.e., towards the *common weal,* is called virtue.

¶7. Upon careful examination of all branches of government, one can easily become convinced that virtue must be a constituent part of every one of them; even justice—which, as stated above, is execution of the laws—owes its existence to virtue alone, because the government is unable to supervise its [implementation] constantly. Virtue, i.e., the people's good habits, always has been and will be the pillar of the state: should virtue cease, no government, no laws will prevent its fall; vice will be enthroned everywhere, sowing enmity among the estates and leading to a neglect, nay even scorn, of the common good; the preference for selfish benefits over all others, ignorance, extortion, baseness, superstition and godlessness, scorn for the fatherland, and indifference to the misfortune of one's neighbor will take the place of love for the common good, enlightenment, honesty, honor, true faith, and sincere attachment to fellow man. The few right-minded men will in vain suffer at this sight and put the blame on the government: their grumblings and reproaches will be quite unjust, for [it is] the ruled [who] are always the cause of such evil. The government is a complex whole whose various parts are directed to a single goal: the common good. Can the government strive for and reach the set goal if we ourselves, who constitute the parts of government, prefer our personal benefit above all, . . . fulfill neither our civic nor our family obligations, and serve our country only for the sake of titles, and frequently for the sake of shameful enrichment at our neighbors' expense? But it is sad to describe the vices that grip us. When evil is in evidence and noticeably on the increase, complaints are fruitless and are the lot of the weak; active opposition to this evil then becomes every citizen's inescapable duty.

¶8. This highest duty of all, and the conviction that there exists no other way to fight against the prevailing evil but to cast aside personal advantage and to unite the forces of virtue against vice, lead us to the organization of a Union of Welfare which all right-minded fellow citizens will no doubt join.

First Book   Aim of the Union of Welfare

¶1. Convinced that good morals are the firm foundation of a nation's virtue and valor, and that all the efforts of the government will fail to reach its goal unless the ruled . . . assist it in this good intent, the Union of Welfare believes that its sacred duty lies in spreading the true rules of morality and enlightenment among our fellow citizens, and in assisting the government in raising Russia to the level of greatness and prosperity to which its Maker has destined it.

¶2. As its aim is the *welfare of society,* the Union does not hide it from right-minded citizens, but in order to avoid the censure of malice and jealousy it must . . . act in secret.

¶3. Intent on strictly observing the rules of justice and virtue in all its actions, the Union does not display those wounds which it cannot undertake to heal right away, for it is guided neither by vainglory nor similar motives, but by a striving for the common welfare.

¶4. The Union hopes for the government's good will, particularly basing itself on the following statement of the Instruction of the late Empress Catherine II:[9] "If their minds are inadequately prepared for the (laws), then take upon yourself the trouble of preparing them for it, and in so doing you will have done much." And in another place: "It is bad policy to correct by law what should have been corrected through manners."

¶5. The following four principal fields constitute the goal of the Union: (1) philanthropy, (2) education, (3) justice, (4) national economy.

First Field: Philanthropy

¶6. The Union supervises all philanthropic institutions in the state, such as hospitals, orphanages, etc., and also those places where man suffers—dungeons, prisons, etc. With an energy that befits its beneficial aim, it endeavors to survey these institutions, improve them as much as possible, and establish new ones. It brings to the government's attention all the defects and abuses that have been noted in those establishments; for the Union is convinced of its [own] genuine sympathy and readiness to proffer a helping hand to all those who suffer. The Union takes particular care also that invalid veterans are assigned to appropriate posts.

Second Field: Education

SECTION 1: DISSEMINATION OF MORAL PRINCIPLES

¶7. The Union takes pains to disseminate genuine principles of virtue among all estates of the population. It reminds and explains to all, their obligations with respect to faith, their neighbors, the fatherland, and established authorities. It points out the unbreakable tie between the people's virtue (i.e., good morals) and its welfare; and it endeavors to eradicate the vices that have entered our hearts, especially the preference for personal . . . advantage, baseness, vile passions, hypocrisy, extortion, and cruelty toward subordinates. In short, by enlightening all concerning their duties,

---

[9] The so-called *Nakaz* given by Catherine II to the Commission on the drafting of a code of laws, which she convened in 1767. The *Nakaz* was a digest of some of the most popular political notions of the *philosophes*. It was frequently used as authority by subsequent Russian reformers and publicists.

the Society tries to reconcile and accord all classes, ranks, and races in the state; it encourages them to strive unanimously toward the government's goal—the common good—so that general popular opinion becomes a tribunal of morality whose beneficent influence would put the finishing touch to the formation of good habits, and in so doing base the welfare and valor of the Russian people on a firm and indestructible foundation.

The Union achieves this end through publication of periodicals consonant with the educational level of each class, the writing and translation of books specifically dealing with man's duties. Personal example and words [of members] must contribute to this aim. In particular, clergy belonging to the Union have an obligation to enlighten their parishioners, not excepting any class, concerning their duties. Even clergymen not belonging to the Union should be encouraged in this sense.

SECTION 2: EDUCATION OF YOUTH

¶8. The education of youth also enters into the permanent goal of the Union of Welfare. All the nation's educational institutions without exception should be under its supervision. It inspects them, improves them, and establishes new ones. In general, with respect to the education of youth, the Union particularly tries to arouse in youth a love for everything virtuous, useful, and beautiful and a scorn for everything vicious and low, so that the strong impulse of the passions be always stopped by the strict but just reminder of an informed reason and conscience.

With respect to private education, the Union should endeavor subtly to induce parents to instill the principles of virtue in their children and support all deserving educators. As to those who, under the guise of educators, worm their way into households to sow dissension and debauchery, the Union not only must drive them out, but, as [they are] corrupters of youth's morals, prevent them from earning their daily bread through the exercise of this craft. In this regard the Union will in particular supervise foreigners who, besides sowing dissension and corruption in the families, instill in the children a scorn for all that is native and an attachment to things foreign. The Union also endeavors to dissuade parents from educating their children in foreign lands. The education of the female sex, as the source of virtue in private education, is also of concern to the Union.

The means used by the Union to this end are: its own example, the spoken word, and periodical publications, in which, among others, should be published the names of recognized good educators and useful [educational] books.

SECTION 3: DISSEMINATION OF KNOWLEDGE

¶9. The Union combats ignorance by all available means and endeavors to instill genuine enlightenment by directing the minds to useful occupations, in particular a knowledge of the fatherland. To this end it writes and translates books, good textbooks as well as books that adorn useful learning. It uses satire to turn [people] away not only from those books that are contrary to the Union's aims, but also from those without any impact. Only the truly beautiful is admissible in literature and everything bad and mediocre is to be cast out.

Third Field: Justice

¶10. A consequence of good morals, justice is without doubt one of the main aspects of national welfare and therefore belongs to the goal of the Union. The Union supervises the execution of government measures, encourages both secular and spiritual officials to fulfill their duties; it keeps informed of all cases under decision and endeavors to induce everybody to follow the path of justice; it supports honest but poor officials; it compensates for losses incurred in the cause of justice; it promotes genuinely deserving individuals; it tries to lead the dishonest and the depraved onto the right path and, failing to do so, at least to deprive them of the opportunity of doing harm. The Union also tries to limit and eradicate the lust for power and disregard for human rights which we acquire in the process of our upbringing and [it endeavors] to convince everybody of the truth that the *nation's common weal absolutely demands the good of the individual, and that every man, whatever his estate, has a right to it.*

Fourth Field: National Economy

¶11. The nation's economy must be a goal of the Union, for it is the foundation of the nation's wealth; through trade and industry it binds together not only all estates, but all the vast territories of the state. The transmission of wealth . . . equalizes the classes and in so doing gives everyone the hope that his industry will allow him to enjoy the parcel of prosperity he has envied in others. The Union pays particular attention to agriculture and all types of useful cultivation of the soil . . . ; it protects all industries useful to the state; it supervises foreign and domestic trade, endeavoring to develop it, and through it vivifies the sterile regions of the fatherland; it patronizes merchants as well as industrialists who have distinguished themselves by laboring for the common good and brings them to the attention of the government, so that they may be rewarded; it singles out honest merchants and tries to turn dishonest ones to their duties; and in general it works for more honesty in trade. The formation of a public Treasury is also of concern to the Union.

Second Book   General Laws of the Union of Welfare

Chapter I: Qualities of the Candidates; General Duties and Rights of Members

1. QUALITIES OF THE CANDIDATES

¶1. Having as its goal the common weal, the Union of Welfare invites to membership all those who by their honest life have earned a good name in society and who, feeling the greatness of the Union's goal, are ready to endure all the hardships that are connected with its attainment.

¶2. The Union has no regard for differences in condition and estate: all Russian citizens—noblemen, clergy, merchants, townspeople, and free men—who agree with the above, confess the Christian faith, and are at least eighteen years old, are admitted to the Union of Welfare.

Note: The Union considers to be Russian citizens those who are born in Russia and who speak Russian. Foreigners who have left their homeland to serve a foreign state, by virtue of this very act, do not deserve confidence and cannot, therefore, be considered Russian citizens. Only those [foreigners] who have rendered important services to our fatherland and are passionately attached to it are deemed by the Union worthy of the name of Russian citizens.

¶3. Women are not admitted to the Union. Efforts should be made, however, to bring them imperceptibly to the organization of philanthropic and *private societies* corresponding to the aim of the Union.

¶4. Anyone known to be a dishonest person and who fails in completely exculpating himself [from this reputation] may not be admitted to the Union of Welfare. In general, all those who are depraved, vicious, and subject to vile passions are precluded from participating in the Union.

2. DUTIES OF THE MEMBERS

¶5. Upon joining the Union, every member, depending on his abilities, must enroll for one of the fields that are defined in the aims of the Union and must contribute as much as possible to its work.

¶6. Every member must unquestioningly obey all lawful orders of the Union's authorities, diligently carry out all assignments, and cheerfully submit to all the rebukes which these authorities may give for failures. . . .

¶7. Members of the Union not only should not avoid public obligations, but as true sons of the fatherland they should accept them with pleasure and carry them out with zeal, and by their blameless conduct, their justice, their nobility, raise the office in the opinion of others.

¶8. In every function, in every post [he occupies], a member of the Union must help others, show respect to virtuous and meritorious individuals, and try to establish contacts with them, always informing the Union. He must also oppose the evil and depraved [individuals] by all means that do not violate public order.

¶9. In public life, too, members of the Union should help each other; members of the nobility must support members from among merchants, townspeople, and husbandmen, while members from these estates must act in similar fashion toward each other and toward noblemen. Members serving in the civil government must speak up for the military and the military must speak up for the civilians; none of this, however, should be contrary to truth or of benefit to vice and crime. In general, everyone should proclaim the verity that true sons of the fatherland must show the same respect to every estate and [form of] service useful to the state, and that those who neglect their duties and prefer vice to virtue only deserve contempt.

¶10. Under penalty of punishment, every member must report to the authorities of the Union all fellow members' illegal and shameful actions.

¶11. The Union members' other obligations derive naturally from its aims. To the extent of his abilities each member must encourage everyone to virtue by his own example, disseminate ideas consonant with the aims of the Union, speak the truth and defend it fearlessly. In short, he must try to build the moral wall which will protect the present as well as future generations from all the miseries of vice, and in so doing erect an everlasting and unshakable foundation for the greatness and welfare of the Russian people.

¶12. After joining the Union every member must contribute yearly one-twenty-fifth of his income to the common treasury. In this respect the Union depends completely on the honesty of every member, for no other feeling than virtue induces all to contribute to the common good.

3. RIGHTS OF THE MEMBERS

¶13. The differences in civil condition and rank are abolished in the Union and replaced by submission to its authorities. This, however, should not preclude normal respect for officials: a member of the Union must always fulfill his public duties most zealously.

¶14. Not only does every member have the right, but he is obliged to participate in the administration and legislation of the Union according to the procedures established by the Constitution. He also has the right to submit in writing his opinion on any subject to the lower as well as higher authorities of the Union.

¶15. No member may be accused on grounds of suspicion alone: he may not be punished until sufficient evidence has been presented against him.

¶16. Any member has the right to organize or be a member of all societies approved by the government, but he must inform the Union of everything that takes place in them and, imperceptibly, he should influence them in the direction of the Union's goals. Members, however, are forbidden to join societies prohibited by the government, because the Union is acting for the good of Russia and, consequently, for the aims of the government and does not wish to subject itself to the latter's suspicion.

¶17. Unless specifically instructed to do so, no one may speak about the work and affairs of the Union with outsiders. Without special permission no one may expound in writing his ideas either against or in favor of the Union. On the contrary, every member should try to avoid any dispute with nonmembers concerning the

Union; but if there is need he must defend the Union and its members with appropriate decorum.

¶18. It should not happen that men, even those of little virtue, who have become fully acquainted with the goals and permanent procedures of the Union would leave it. But there are fainthearted [men] who lead an almost vegetative life, who are responsible neither for their good nor for their bad actions, and who from weakness and indecision [may] have joined the Union in a moment's longing for virtue, and then, spurred on by no one, have returned to their natural state of complete moral inactivity. [These men] may be tormented by their momentary decisiveness; for this reason, in consideration of the sickly predisposition of these unfortunate men, the Union allows them to withdraw, on condition, however, that they keep secret everything they know about it.

Chapter II: Members' Admission, Rewards, Penalties, Expulsion

¶19. Only those who possess the qualities defined in the first four articles of Chapter I may be admitted to membership.

¶20. Before admission to the Union, every candidate must indicate whom he can influence sufficiently in favor of the Union's aims. . . .

¶21. Persons who are known to all for their truly good qualities and unquestioned influence may dispense with such a statement.

¶22. Upon admission, every member signs the following statement: "Relying on the assurance that nothing in the aims of the Union of Welfare is contrary to religion, the fatherland, or my public duties, I, the undersigned, pledge on my honor, not to divulge, and particularly not to criticize these [aims and by-laws] if, after they have been read to me, I do not like them and [decide] not to enter the Union."

¶23. If after reading the first part of the Constitution of the Union he wishes to join, he must sign the following statement: "Finding the aims and by-laws of the Union of Welfare in full accord with my own principles, I, the undersigned, pledge to participate actively in the Union's administration and work, to submit to its by-laws and its established authorities; in addition, I give my word of honor that even if I leave the Union, either voluntarily or under compulsion, I shall not criticize it and still less act against it. If

[I act] to the contrary I voluntarily submit to the contempt of all right-minded men."

¶24. No one can be excused from giving his word of honor and signature.

¶25. The names of members who have rendered important services to the Union by zealously fulfilling their duties are entered in a *book of honor* and their accomplishments are broadcast throughout the Union.

¶26. The member who neglects his obligations first receives a gentle admonition and if he does not change his behavior he is expelled from the Union.

¶27. He who acts against the aims of the Union, receives first a gentle warning, first privately then in the presence of witnesses; on the third time, he is expelled from the Union.

¶28. The names of members who have been expelled from the Union are entered into a *book of shame*.

Third Book   Organization of the Union

Chapter I: Organization of the Principal Union

¶1. The union of the first members who have agreed to act according to the aforementioned principles is called the *Principal Union*.

¶2. From there the spreading of the Union to all parts of the state has its beginnings.

¶3. From its midst, the Principal Union elects six members, to whom the main administration of the Union is entrusted.

COUNCIL OF THE PRINCIPAL UNION

¶4. Five of these members are called Assessors, and the sixth, Keeper, whose duty it is to supervise the keeping of the Union's decisions. The five Assessors and the Keeper constitute the *Council of the Principal Union*.

¶5. Under the Keeper's supervision, the Council of the Principal Union [first] elects one of the Assessors to be President of the Council for two months, and then designates by lot three Presidents for the following six months.

¶6. The President of the Council is called Head.

¶7. But so that other members of the Principal Union may participate in the main administration, every four months two Assessors designated by lot withdraw from the Principal Council and rejoin the ranks of the Principal Union. The Keeper withdraws at the same time as the last Assessor.

¶8. As the members of the Council withdraw, they are replaced by others from among the remaining members of the Principal Union.

PRINCIPAL BOARD

¶9. These other members, together with the Principal Council, form the *Principal Board*.

¶10. The Head of the Principal Council presides also over the Principal Board. The Assessors also belong to it and hold first place.

¶11. Every member of the Principal Board must set up unions or assemblies acting in the sense of the Society and becoming part of it. At first these members are alone in spreading the Union. The Societies established by them are called Boards.

PLENIPOTENTIARIES OF THE PRINCIPAL UNION

¶12. Outsiders enjoying the confidence of the Principal Union may be given membership and appointed as its *Plenipotentiaries* for the establishment of Boards in the regions where they reside.

ACTIVITIES OF THE PRINCIPAL COUNCIL

¶13. The Principal Council: (1) preserves unity of action among the Boards and maintains the necessary communication between them; (2) apportions assignments and activities useful to the Union among the members and coordinates all actions. It meets at least once a month to receive reports from the founders of Boards. In a general way, it holds the *executive power*.

ACTIVITIES OF THE PRINCIPAL BOARD

In the Principal Board are vested: the legislative power, the supreme judiciary, and the appointment of officials.

¶14. He who without due cause refuses to establish a Board or some society in the sense of the Union is immediately expelled from the Principal Union.

LEGISLATIVE CHAMBER

¶15. Finally, the Principal Union appoints a special *Temporary Legislative Chamber* for the examination, interpretation, and execution of the by-laws of the Union. This Temporary Legislative Chamber may not, however, make changes in the goals of the Union: *actions of public virtue* and the *striving for the good* will always be the traits of the whole Union. If the Principal Board approves the work of the Temporary Legislative Chamber, then its laws will be in force temporarily, until confirmation by the Supreme Administration which will be set up only when the Union has been completely organized. The Principal Board approves laws by majority vote.

Chapter II: Organization of Boards

¶16. Articles 11, 12, and 14 stated that every member of the Principal Union must establish a Board. The membership of the Boards should be no less than ten and no more than twenty. There are Active, Secondary, and Main Boards.

ACTIVE BOARDS

¶17. As long as it has less than ten members a Board is considered inactive. As soon as it has ten members it is called an *Active Board* and receives a copy of the first part of the Union's Constitution.

¶18. The Principal Union, however, has the right to make exceptions to this rule for the sake of the Union's more rapid growth.

¶19. Half of the legal number of members of a Board (i.e., five) absolutely must be residents of the place where the Board is established.

SECONDARY BOARDS

¶20. Every Board has the right to establish another, which is called a *Secondary Board.*

¶21. The founding Board has the right to give instructions to the Secondary Board and in general see to it that it acts in the sense of the Union.

¶22. The Secondary Board, except in unforeseen cases, never communicates with the Principal Board, but solely with the Board that has founded it.

¶23. If a Secondary Board itself establishes another Board it becomes independent from its founding Board. But the Secondary Board must consist of no less than ten members. Except for members of the Principal Board, no one may found Boards without permission from the Principal Board or the Council of his own Board.

MAIN BOARDS

¶24. A Board that has founded three Secondary Boards or Voluntary Associations receives the name of *Main Board* and along with it a copy of the final organization of the Union, i.e., the second part of its Constitution.

¶25. Every Board established by a member of the Principal Union must grow to a membership of at least ten within six months. Otherwise it is closed and the Council of the Principal Union merges it with another or distributes its members among other Boards.

¶26. After the first ten Active Boards have been established, the Principal Board will be replenished from their membership as provided in articles 7 and 8. Every four months, one-third of the members of the Principal Union, designated by lot, retire from it and are distributed among the Boards. . . .

Chapter III: Administration of the Boards

¶27. Each founder of an Active Board is himself its President and Keeper for the first three months. If he withdraws during this period, the Board immediately elects these two officials. The President of the Board has the right to select a Secretary.

COUNCIL OF THE BOARD

¶28. Upon expiration of the aforesaid three months, every Board with ten members elects one Elder, and every Board with twenty, two—in addition to the Keeper whom every Board must have, regardless of the membership. These elected [men] constitute the *Council of the Board.*

ACTIVITIES OF THE COUNCIL

¶29. The Council of the Board's functions are: (1) Administration of the business of its Secondary Boards and Voluntary Associations. (2) Carrying out of assignments on instruction from the Principal Council of the Union. (3) Its presiding Elder is President of the Board. (4) The Council has the right to censure for disorder.

(5) It grants permission to establish a Board and issues to its founder a copy of the first part of the Union's Constitution. (6) It keeps safely, on the responsibility of all members of the Council: (i) the list of the members of the Board, of the Secondary Boards, and of the Voluntary Associations subordinated to it; (ii) the book of signatures of those who have joined; (iii) a copy of the by-laws of the Union given to the Board.

ACTIVITIES OF THE BOARDS

The Board itself is concerned with: legislation, punishing guilty members and Elders, deciding business submitted by Secondary Boards.

ELECTIONS

¶30. During the first two years, Elders and Keepers are elected for *six months,* subsequently for *one year.*

¶31. During the first two years, upon expiration of three months one Elder withdraws from the Council by lot. The remaining Elder and Keeper withdraw after six months.

¶32. After expiration of the first two years, one Elder withdraws by lot every six months, and upon expiration of a year the other Elder and Keeper.

¶33. Members of the Council who have withdrawn are replaced by election.

¶34. Elections take place in the presence of all available members and of the Keeper who, on this occasion, has no voice.

¶35. Members absent on Union business may send in their vote in writing to the Council of the Board or entrust it to another member by informing the Keeper. . . .

¶36. No member shall stand in as a proxy for more than one member.

¶37. Elections are decided on the basis of *majority.*

¶38. Reelections of members to the posts they have vacated are decided by a two-thirds majority of members voting.

CORRESPONDENCE

¶39. Communications between Boards and the Principal Union are in the form of private letters between the Elder or Keeper and the Head, or an Assessor, or the Keeper of the Principal Council.

Chapter IV: Admission to Membership

¶40. As long as the Board has less than ten members, its founder alone has the right to admit [new] members; but as soon as the membership reaches ten, the right of admission passes to the Board.

¶41. In the latter case, one of the members nominates the candidate whom he knows to the Council, describing his qualities, and also guaranteeing their accuracy.

¶42. The Council informs all members available about the nominee. Whoever is against admission must give his reasons to the Council within three days. If he gives no reason, his opposition is disregarded and at the next meeting of the Council the matter is settled.

¶43. If an Elder or the Keeper find the opposition justified, the nominee is temporarily rejected; if two members of the Council oppose the nomination, the candidate is permanently barred from the Board.

¶44. If there is no opposition, or if it has been found insufficient, the Council admits the candidate to the Board's membership according to established procedure.

¶45. Having given the pledges mentioned earlier, the candidate is admitted and presents to the Board a list of all his acquaintances who might enter the Union. This list should indicate their residence, age, rank, and title. He informs the Board separately about those who by virtue of their talent could be of particular use to the Union. These descriptions are retained by the Keeper of the Board, who transmits a copy of them to higher authorities.

¶46. The Council of the Principal Board gives permission to establish an Active Board only if it receives ten signatures from the founder.

¶47. At the opportune moment, on the basis of the lists received, the Council of the Principal Board gives to one member permission to contact the talented outsider and give him a copy of the first part of the Union's Constitution to read; but first he must secure the signature to the required statement.

Chapter V: Voluntary Associations

¶48. *Voluntary Associations* in the Union of Welfare are all societies that share its aims but are not part of it.

¶49. To found and maintain them is considered a particularly meritorious action and the names of members of the Union who do so are entered in the book of honor.

¶50. However, permission of the Principal Union is necessary for the establishment of such associations.

¶51. The purpose of these associations, as well as their organization, membership, and activities are left to the discretion of their founder.

¶52. These associations should bring about and strengthen concord and unanimity, the desire to share useful ideas, knowledge of civic duties, and love of country.

Chapter VI: Duties of Officers and Conduct of Business

¶53. The presiding Elder convokes the Council and the Board, distributes business among the members of the latter, communicates with the Principal Union, informs the Principal Council of the Board's actions.

¶54. The Keeper of the Board supervises the members' morals and the implementation of the Union's Constitution. He makes accusations and representations. He stops the Council's and Board's actions when he finds them incompatible with the laws and aims of the Union. He remonstrates with those who neglect their duties; in short, the Keeper supervises everything that takes place in the Board and with its members; and he is held accountable should he fail to stop any action incompatible with the aims of the Union. He is in communication with the Principal Council.

MEMBERS

¶55. Each member does all that is in accordance with the aims of the Union and enrolls in the field [of activity] most in accord with his own activities, talents, and his service experience.

¶56. The activity of a member is not limited to the field in which he enrolls; in addition to the business connected with his chosen field, anyone may participate in the affairs of other fields.

¶57. Every member should inform his Board of the abuses and deficiencies he has noted in the fatherland, so as to put an end to them. If the Board itself is unable to help, it reports to the Principal Council so that the latter may inform the government and thereby put an end to the evil or disorder.

DECISIONS

¶58. All decisions in the Union are taken by majority vote.

SENTENCES

¶59. Sentences, too, are taken by majority vote.

¶60. Sentences of expulsion from the Union of a guilty member are submitted for confirmation to the Principal Board.

¶61. Dues set by the Constitution constitute the Treasury of the Union, which is kept in the Board by members elected for this purpose and used for the Board's business by decision of the Board or its Council.

¶62. The Principal Board may demand part of the Treasury of the Boards for the common needs of the Union.

¶63. The Board's Treasury also assists needy members who are worthy of its help. The Keeper has to ascertain the needs of members of the Board. Help from fellow members can never be a cause of shame for the recipient; but to leave a member without help is shameful for the Union. . . .

PLENIPOTENTIARIES OF THE PRINCIPAL UNION

¶65. Plenipotentiaries of the Principal Union set up Boards and maintain communication between them and the Principal Board. A Board established by a Plenipotentiary communicates with the Principal Board directly only if it is given permission to do so.

¶66. Plenipotentiaries of the Principal Union may select assistants from among members and give them permission to establish Boards in the area under their jurisdiction.

¶67. As frequently as possible they must give detailed information on their activities to the Principal Council, from which they also receive their instructions.

¶68. In everything they must act according to the Constitution, from which nobody is permitted to deviate.

¶69. The Principal Board may confer power to inspect the established Boards.

CONCLUSION

¶70. Everything set forth in this Constitution may be complemented and clarified, but it cannot be modified, for the aim of the Union, i.e., the eradication of vice and the spreading of virtue, always remains immutable. Clarification and addition are exclusively a function of the Principal Board.

Fourth Book   Apportioning of Activities

¶1. Members belonging to a particular field are entrusted by the Union with the supervision of everything in the fatherland that pertains to their field. They do everything to further the Union's goal and they inform the Union of conditions, so that the latter can take all appropriate measures and inform the government of everything that needs correction. The object and action of every field are defined below.

¶2. No member will report abuses he has noted in the fatherland privately to the government, for [such a report] is a special act of the administration of the Union, which takes the measures most appropriate to this end. Members of the Union may, however, personally call abuses to the attention of the local authorities.

¶3. The Union publishes nothing without the consent of its administration; but a member is not forbidden to publish in his own name works that the Union does not publish or those he wishes to publish personally.

¶4. The Union gives assignments to members in accordance with the activity of the field or section in which they are enrolled. However, a member may also take on an assignment that does not correspond to his chosen field or section; for it is up to him whether he belongs to a particular field or section, or to several, or to all at once.

¶5. As soon as a Board has been set up somewhere, its members select their work in accordance with the field or division in which they are enrolled and inform the Council of the Board of their activities, so that the latter may report on the progress to the administration of the Union.

¶6. The Council of the Board immediately submits to the Principal Council detailed information on the membership's choice of fields or sections, on the work they have undertaken, and on their success.

¶7. If, in distributing assignments to the Boards, the Principal Council does not indicate by name the members to be entrusted with their execution, then the Council of the Board itself makes the [individual] assignments, taking into account the members' talents and their choice of fields.

¶8. The Council of the Board informs the Principal Council of who was given [each particular] assignment.

First Field: Philanthropy

¶9. This virtue is a quality that distinguishes not only the true Christian but also very uneducated people. There is no man in the world completely indifferent to his neighbor's misfortune and who would not be stirred to compassion by the sight of a creature like himself in extreme want. When those with bad qualities are not without this virtue, how much more should it fire a Union which has as its purpose to labor for the welfare of its fellow citizens? At the sight of an unfortunate, everyone will give help, to the beggar [everybody gives] alms. But can such assistance, given only once, satisfy forever him who receives it? Moreover, how many worthless individuals do we see among them, who, in order to indulge their laziness, wander about the world collecting their subsistence from donations? Whereas if they [displayed] industry they in turn could be useful to their country and to other genuinely unfortunate men. Instead, they are a burden to their fatherland, they stimulate in others the wish to be idle and destroy the very roots of morality. To eradicate this evil and replace it with all the opposite virtues is the concern of this field and of the members enrolled in it. To this end the Union supervises with ever-watchful eye all those institutions . . . belonging to this field and labors for their improvement.

¶10. The Union invites to this field residents of towns enjoying wealth and general esteem; administrators of philanthropic institutions, jails, and reformatories; as well as members practicing the medical arts.

¶11. The members in this field urge landowners to turn their peasants away from vagabondage, and they subject to their fellow citizens' judgment those who have many [vagabond peasants], to induce them to take measures to stop idle vagabondage.

¶12. In general they endeavor to induce the landowners to treat their peasants well by pointing out that: *subjects [serfs] are men like others and that there are no special rights in the world permitting lords to deal cruelly with those in their power.*

¶13. They persuade compatriots to establish philanthropic societies and institutions and to join those already in existence.

¶14. They provide idle vagabonds with work by trying to place them according to their talents and by establishing work houses where they could find sure and adequate subsistence.

¶15. They set up shelters for those unable to support themselves by their work. Among the latter are many old and invalid warriors who, after spending the blooming years of their youth in defense of the fatherland, are not allowed to spend the remainder of their days in peace, and in most cases are forced to find their subsistence by begging. The grateful fatherland must show these men its appreciation of the services they have rendered and soothe their old age. The Union endeavors to place these [men] in quiet government and private posts and by common effort to establish peaceful shelters for them.

¶16. In provincial capitals and large towns members of the Union [will] establish *bureaus* to which all free men wishing placement and work will be invited to come. These bureaus find them work and positions according to their talents, paying particular attention to their conduct. Those proven to be of bad conduct will be required to mend their ways and be provided with the means for doing it. If they persist in their bad ways and morals, they are turned away. The managers of these bureaus are selected with the consent of the Board Council in the city, and it is to these that they account for the execution of the assignment they have undertaken.

¶17. The Union entrusts its members in this field with the supervision of all philanthropic institutions and of all places where men suffer. The members will send descriptions of these places to the administration of the Union and report all deficiencies and abuses they have noticed.

¶18. In their travels, members in this field [will] visit institutions pertaining to the field and report on their condition to the Union.

¶19. Members in this field [will] promote vaccination against smallpox as an important preventive measure to safeguard the life of infants.

¶20. They also endeavor to find means for improving philanthropic institutions in the fatherland.

¶21. To the extent possible, they visit and describe such institutions abroad.

¶22. They publish periodicals and disseminate works already available in this field.

Second Field: Education

SECTION 1: DISSEMINATION OF MORAL PRINCIPLES

¶23. The very aim of the Union is the dissemination of principles of morality and virtue, and consequently, it is a duty for every member. But as members in other fields are particularly concerned with improvements in the fields of philanthropy, justice, and national economy, the dissemination of these principles becomes a special obligation of members in the field of education. The labors and unpleasantness connected with it will be requited with interest by the importance of this glorious and voluntarily accepted burden.

¶24. The Union invites to this section clergymen and all those who by virtue of their position in society can affect morality most.

¶25. The principles adopted by the Union are disseminated through personal example, and through the spoken and written word.

Personal example

¶26. Every member of the Union, and more particularly a member in the second field, must set an example to his fellow citizens [by doing the following]: (1) Fulfill his family as well as his public obligations in a superior manner. (2) Disparage the vicious, scorn the unworthy, and promote the virtuous in every place and to the extent of his abilities. (3) In all his actions display his nobility and the elevation of his soul. . . . (4) Not waste his time in the false pleasures of high society, but use his hours of leisure . . . in useful occupations or in conversation with right-minded individuals. (5) Be particularly attached to everything native and prove this attachment by his actions. (6) Be kindhearted and humane in the government of his subjects, and by the example of his honest life incite them to virtue. In short, *in his thoughts and through his important as well as trivial actions, he must raise himself above the crowd of fickle, thoughtless, and vice-ridden people.*

¶27. So that genuinely good examples have their desired effect, every member, and especially a member in the second field, ought to [do the following]: (1) Make an effort to find out the qualities of his acquaintances and strengthen his bonds with the most virtuous; earn their confidence and keep an eye on their actions, bend them to the ways of virtue. (2) Establish new ties with people who are capable of feeling the necessity of virtue, and after earning their confidence and esteem confirm them in the principles of virtue by his own example. (3) Act in this manner particularly with respect to young people who, because they have not yet received a thorough education, enter onto the stage of public life with a readiness to absorb good and bad influences with equal avidity.

The spoken word

¶28. Every member in the second field must endeavor to exalt virtue, debase vice, and show contempt for weakness.

¶29. By his words he must try to be of substantial use and not merely scintillating.

¶30. He must broadcast the [following] truths: (1) False pleasures and the various objects of human passion, of necessity remove one from happiness. (2) The surest and only means to attain happiness is to fulfill one's duty toward others. (3) Among one's duties to others the most important are those concerning the fatherland; to strive for the common good is the concern of every citizen. (4) Only with the help of faith can man overcome his passions, overcome hostile circumstances, and thereby walk in virtue's path. (5) Our faith consists not only of external rituals, but of our very deeds. (6) The sacred precepts of religion not only do not take us from our social duties; [but] on the contrary, the true Christian is the best family man and the most loyal son and most active servant of the fatherland.

¶31. He [the member] must endeavor: (1) To demonstrate that the personal good is inseparable from the common weal and that the so-called personal advantages are meaningless. (2) To convince that the satisfaction of passions is illusory and has bad results. (3) To unmask the baseness of hypocrisy and its conflict with true faith. (4) To call attention . . . to the horrible consequences of extortion and to the necessity of opposing this evil. (5) to prove to everybody that it is dishonest to be cruel to subordinates, for even without oppression their fate deserves not only compassion but also all possible efforts for amelioration. (6) To ridicule today's all too common search for pleasure and its objects. . . . (7) To demonstrate the stupidity and bad effects of being attached to foreign things and also to make efforts to convince that a virtuous citizen must always prefer the useful to the pleasant and the native to the foreign. (8) To call the parents' attention to the education of their children. (9) To turn the female sex from idle pleasures and provide it with a new field of endeavor in the dissemination of elevated sentiments, such as love of country and of genuine enlightenment.

¶32. The member must direct his young acquaintances to useful occupations, establish societies with or for them, occupy them with various subjects, but so that all their occupations, actions, and reflections have one result: the *common good*.

¶33. Members owning estates must try to have learned and virtuous priests who, by their example and teaching, would endeavor to lead their parishioners to virtue's path.

¶34. Chosen by the government itself to disseminate moral principles, members from the clergy must make special efforts to enlighten laymen in the spirit of the Union. They also supervise the behavior of clergy who are not members of the Union, communicating their observations to the Union, so that the latter may support the work of the virtuous and destroy the intrigues of the vicious.

The written word

¶35. It is the duty of the member in the second field to join, with the Union's permission, all the government-approved societies caring for morality and inform the Union of all the actions [of these societies], so that the Union may coordinate its aims with theirs.

¶36. All works published by members in this field must have as their main concern the promotion of virtue.

¶37. The section disseminating moral principles, combining its forces, engages [in the following]: (1) Translation and composition of good moral books. (2) Examination of already existing ones. (3) Publication of a periodical in which moral problems are discussed, the virtues of great men described, etc., and in which the prevailing prejudices are satirized. . . .

SECTION 2: EDUCATION OF YOUTH

¶38. Members in this section must endeavor to obtain the most reliable information on educational institutions in the state, report it to the Union, and submit plans to correct the defects that have been noted. Members inform the Union about particularly good as well as bad educators, so that the Union may further the promotion of the ones and the demotion of the others.

¶39. Through their acquaintance or service [the members] must try to secure participation in the administration of educational institutions, so as to impart the proper direction to the education of youth and [see to it] that educational institutions, in disseminating useful knowledge, pay the greatest attention to the pupils' moral formation.

Personal example

¶40. To the extent possible, [members] have themselves an obligation to establish institutions of learning for the education of young people; these institutions must be oriented toward the aims of the Union.

¶41. To the extent possible, members owning estates must establish schools in their villages and see to it that they operate properly.

¶42. Concerning private education, members who are active in it—i.e., bring up their own or other people's children—must strive to impart to [their pupils] the principles of virtue and faith, fire them with love of country and of everything truly good and great, and provide them with the most useful knowledge. In short, prepare them to live like virtuous men, and devoted and useful citizens.

¶43. In bringing up [children] they should as much as possible avoid everything foreign, so that the sacred feelings of love of one's own country may not be stymied by even the smallest infatuation with foreign things.

The spoken word

¶44. In speaking on education the members must endeavor to convince [people of the following]: (1) How strong the influence of education is on man's entire life. (2) How little attention is nowadays paid to genuine education and how little it is replaced by the glitter that attempts to cover up the young people's nullity. (3) That the main object of education must be morality and that nothing ought to be discarded that may serve to stimulate love for every-thing truly good and great in a youth. (4) That the most powerful means for the formation of a young man's morality is to confirm in him a loyal adherence to the principles of religion. (5) That the subject matter of education must be restricted to those fields that contribute to the formation of the mind and heart, i.e., not to pre-pare the young person for a specific calling, but [to prepare him] in general for the calling of a citizen and virtuous man. (6) These sub-jects are: for the formation of the mind, exact sciences; for the formation of the heart, history; for the formation of a person for the calling of citizen and for illustrating his duties, political sciences. (7) How essential it is for everybody's own happiness to take care of his children's education and how sweet these parental cares. . . . (8) That the best and most esteemed calling for the female sex is the education of children in accordance with the principles of virtue and faith.

The written word

¶45. Members in this field must spread the same truths in their writings.

¶46. The section on education of youth must engage in: (1) The description of educational institutions, both native and foreign, showing their advantages and drawbacks. (2) The composition and translation of books on the education of youth and the elaboration of the best means for public and private education. (3) The compo-sition and translation of textbooks in various disciplines. (4) The publication of a periodical containing: (i) information on new insti-tutions at home and abroad pertaining to education; (ii) articles on education and related subjects; (iii) reviews of published textbooks.

SECTION 3: DISSEMINATION OF KNOWLEDGE

¶47. Taking into consideration that among the knowledge which the human mind is capable of acquiring, the most useful is that which best enables one's heart and reason to contribute to the common good, the Union endeavors through this section to dis-seminate those sciences which enlighten man on his duties and assist him in fulfilling them.

Personal example

¶48. Members in this section are selected from among those addicted to study and they must give preference to the most useful fields and to those best suited to the calling of citizen.

¶49. Members engaged in literature must give to their works the imprint of the beautiful, not forgetting that the truly beautiful arouses in us elevated feelings which carry us away to the good.

¶50. Members must endeavor to encourage their acquaintances to engage in useful studies, help them in their work, turn them away from the low and mediocre, and direct to the truly beautiful those possessed with literary gifts.

The spoken word

¶51. In talking about learned subjects [the members ought to]: (1) Praise the useful and the beautiful, scorn the mediocre, and combat the evil. (2) Show the necessity of knowledge, the lowliness of ignorance, and the distinction between pedantry and genuine enlightenment. (3) Pay attention to the state and orientation of contemporary enlightenment. (4) Explain the needs for a national literature, defend good works, point out the defects of bad ones. (5) Demonstrate that genuine eloquence does not consist in pompously wrapping meaningless ideas in high words, but in the modest expression of useful, elevated, genuinely experienced thoughts. (6) Convince that the power and charm of poetry does not consist in the sound of words, in grandiloquent ideas, or in obscurity of exposition, but in vivid writing, modest expressions, and above all in an unassuming description of elevated feelings that lead to the good. (7) [Stress] that descriptions of an object or of a feeling which debase, instead of stimulate, lofty thoughts are always unworthy of poetry's gift, whatever their prettiness.

The written word

¶52. Members in this section should broadcast the same truths in their written works.

¶53. With the knowledge of the Union, members should try to join all learned societies and orient them toward truly enlightened goals.

¶54. The section on the dissemination of knowledge works at the following: (1) Composes and translates books in the following branches of learning: (i) speculative disciplines, to the extent that they are useful to the citizens; (ii) natural sciences, in particular their applicability in the fatherland; (iii) political sciences, selecting what is most pertinent to the fatherland; (iv) literature, paying particular attention to enriching and purifying the language. (2) Reviews the best-known books in the various branches of useful knowledge. (3) Publishes a periodical to contain: (i) discussions of various learned subjects; (ii) information of discoveries; (iii) reviews of books published; (iv) small compositions and poetry.

¶55. This section endeavors to find the means to give the correct orientation to the fine arts . . . to strengthen our virtues and elevate our moral being.

Third Field: Justice

¶56. All branches of the country's administration are under the supervision of members in this field.

¶57. Members not only do not refuse or avoid offices, especially elective offices from the nobility, but on the contrary seek them; through their own blameless and selfless service careers they elevate and maintain the importance and dignity of these offices. Strict and zealous execution of his service or government duties distinguishes the member of the Union of Welfare.

¶58. Members supervise officials who are not members of the Union and with the Union's help encourage honest attitudes in service and all public business. . . .

¶59. They concern themselves with all matters that are decided in government offices and military courts, and orient everything toward justice.

¶60. They bring about harmony between various peoples, estates, conditions, and services in the fatherland by pointing out that all are equally useful, and they orient them all into one direction: the welfare of Russia.

¶61. This field needs more members than all others, for it encompasses more activities which are fettered by the exactions and oppressions of many people. Members in this field abandon neither rank nor service posts and try not to falter in their chosen path. The Union invites to this field: (1) Those who cannot actively participate in philanthropy and education because of: (i) their remoteness from those places that radiate enlightenment, e.g., the capitals and big cities; (ii) their unsteady residence, due to their service position and occupation. (2) Those who live in big cities and capitals and participate in various branches of the administration. (3) Those who are in service somewhere. (4) Those who enjoy general esteem. This is the reason why many military personnel, retired persons who live in provincial districts and serve in the capacity of elected officials from the nobility, and others, are enrolled in this field.

¶62. Members in this field: (1) Attack the slavish fawning and lust for power of many of our compatriots. (2) Arouse public opinion against officials who, in violation of their sacred duty, destroy that which has been entrusted to their safeguard and oppress and ruin those whom their duty commands to protect. (3) Eradicate the abuses that have crept into the civil service, especially in elective and judiciary institutions. (4) Praise landowners renowned for the good treatment of their subordinates. (5) Extirpate the selling of serfs into the army; in general discourage the sale of single persons by trying to implant the notion that men are not commodities and that only people who have not been illuminated by the light of Christianity are to be forgiven if they consider beings alike to themselves as property to be disposed of at will. (6) Set up as an example to others officials who zealously fulfill their duty. (7) In general, direct their activities toward correcting all abuses, raising the just in public esteem, compensating those exploited and oppressed innocently. In short, to the extent of his powers, every member endeavors to give everyone his due.

¶63. [The members in this field] try to persuade the nobility in the [local] districts to set adequate salaries for elected officials, to deprive the poor nobles of their usual excuse that their estate is too small—[an excuse] resulting in that many, who do not have the proper education, far from considering the taking of bribes a crime, think it to be a necessary and lawful thing. In fact they serve not for the sake of their fellow citizens' welfare, but to make a living and even enrich themselves. As such a common custom sets a horrible example of immorality and brings irreparable harm to the country, all members of the Union, in whatever field, who possess land and property must endeavor to deflect their fellow citizens from the aforementioned evil.

¶64. Members of justice report to the Union respectable and honest people whom the Union encourages or assists in case of need, and defends if they suffer persecution for the sake of justice. And the Union calls their merit to the attention of the government. The members also report to the Union dishonest people in order to deprive them of the means of doing harm.

¶65. These members [of justice] are deemed to have been instituted by the Union to safeguard justice. They always act, speak, and judge rightly, are not afraid of the opinion of the timid, do not feel unhappy when they suffer for the sake of truth. Strong by virtue of their rightness, they are strengthened still more by their tight bonds and the Union's and the government's special protection.

¶66. They establish Voluntary Associations aimed at what is just and at destroying vice and injustice. These Associations should collect public funds for the compensation of losses suffered for the sake of justice.

¶67. One could add much to these activities worthy of attracting the labors and efforts of members in the field of justice. But we leave this concern to time and the Union's success. Better describe what has been done already for the good of the country rather than point out what has still to be done.

Fourth Field: National Economy

¶68. With this field the Union shows its concern for discovering the permanent principles of public wealth, about which there has been so much discussion for so many centuries. It renders assistance in improving all sorts of useful enterprises and it endeavors to create public confidence; it opposes harmful monopolies concentrated in a few hands.

¶69. Invited [to membership] in this field are: (1) Members engaged in public economy and industry. (2) Employees in commerce and state economy.

¶70. [Members] endeavor above all to introduce strict honesty in trade, for in its absence there will always be distrust.

¶71. [Members] inform their compatriots of new and useful discoveries by means of books and articles in periodicals.

¶72. [Members] try to find ways to compensate those who have suffered ruinous losses because of unfortunate circumstances.

¶73. Members in trade do not violate government regulations but, on the contrary, endeavor to eradicate the abuses that have penetrated the customs houses and report them to the Union.

¶74. To the extent possible, members in this field try to establish in their places of residence insurance offices to make compensation for accidents, such as losses from fire. . . . Nonmembers may participate in these insurance offices, but unless they are Voluntary Associations their administration depends on the Union.

¶75. Members in this field establish Voluntary Associations for the promotion of agriculture and other kinds of enterprises.

¶76. Members in this field are also engaged, in their places of residence, in making descriptions of the fatherland, its industries, trade, the condition of agriculture, etc.

¶77. Additions may be made to all these fields and still their varied activities cannot be described in detail. . . . In any case, whatever his office or calling, a member of the Union of Welfare must remember that he has promised to contribute zealously and tirelessly to the *good of the fatherland* and to act in all his doings in accordance with this generous aim. His reward is the esteem of his compatriots.

> No man, having put his hand to the plow, and
> looking back, is fit for the kingdom of God.
> [Luke 9:62]

IV

The Northern Society

The Northern Society was fated to play the major role in the actual events of December 14, 1825, on Senate Square. Actually, it was poorly prepared for this part. One of the reasons for the poor showing made by the Northern Society on the fateful day of the uprising was failure of leadership. Prince Sergei Petrovich Trubetskoi was to have been proclaimed dictator on December 14, but he lost his nerve and kept out of the limelight. He had, however, written a proclamation embodying some of the general principles set forth by Murav'ev, intended to serve as directive for a provisional administration. The latter was to be headed by a few prominent dignitaries who had the reputation (not really deserved) of agreeing with the Decembrists and of being liberals.

The members of the Society, who were predominantly from the upper nobility and elite officer corps, held rather moderate views. The most comprehensive statement of the Northern Society's political orientation is to be found in Nikita M. Murav'ev's draft for a Constitution. As can be seen, it provides for a constitutional monarchy and a federal organization of the Empire, and in many respects clearly follows in the footsteps of the Constitution of the United States. The heightened nationalism and more sophisticated historical consciousness of the post-Napoleonic generation found expression in Murav'ev's terminology, which was derived from medieval Russian institutions. The Constitution is sometimes referred to as the "Green Book," since it was written in a notebook bound in green. The project remained incomplete in both of its drafts.

A Proclamation by Prince Sergei Petrovich Trubetskoi,
From *Vosstanie Dekabristov*, I (1925), 107-8.

> Lord, Save thy people and bless thine inheritance!
>
> [Ps. 28:9]

The Manifesto of the Senate makes known:

1. The abolition of the previous government.
2. The establishment of a temporary [government] until the formation of a permanent [one] by elected deputies.
3. Freedom of the press, and hence the abolition of censorship.
4. Freedom of worship to all faiths.
5. Abolition of property rights over persons.
6. Equality before the law of all estates and, therefore, abolition of Military Tribunals and all types of Judicial Commissions; all pending cases are to be transferred to the jurisdiction of the nearest civil court.
7. Proclamation of every citizen's right to engage in any [occupation] he wishes; and, therefore, the nobleman, the merchant, the burgher, or the peasant has the same right: to enter into the military and civil services and into the clergy; to engage in wholesale and retail trade by paying the established dues; to acquire all kinds of property, such as land [and] houses in towns and villages; to enter into all types of mutual contracts; to litigate in courts.
8. The remission of the capitation tax and of arrears on it.
9. Abolition of monopolies, as for example on salt, the sale of liquor, etc., and therefore, the establishment of the freedom to distill [alcohol] and to mine salt [on condition

of] payment of dues proportional to the amount of salt
and liquor produced.

10. Abolition of conscription and military colonies.

11. Decrease in the length of service for the lower ranks. [New]
    definition of its length will follow the equalization of
    military service obligations for all classes.

12. Retirement of all lower ranks with fifteen years of service,
    without exception.

13. Establishment of township [*volost'*], district [*uezd*], pro-
    vincial [*gubernskii*], and regional [*oblast'*] administrations,
    and of the procedures for the election of members of these
    administrations who are to replace all the officials hereto-
    fore appointed by the civil government.

14. Public trials.

15. The introduction of jurors into civil and criminal courts.

A government of two or three persons is established;[1] all
branches of the central administration, i.e., Ministries, Council [of
State], Committee of Ministers, Army, Navy, in short, all the executive, but not the legislative or judiciary, powers are subordinated to
it. For the judiciary, the Ministry [of Justice] remains subordinated
to the Provisional Government. Cases not decided in lower courts will
be adjudicated as a last resort by the Criminal Department of the
Senate, to which a Civil Department will be added, with the same
membership as now until the establishment of a Permanent Government.

The Provisional Government is charged with bringing about
the following:

1. Equalization of the rights of all classes.

2. The formation of local township, district, provincial, and
   regional administrations.

---

[1] This refers to the Northern Society's plan to proclaim a provisional government. Among its members were to be Mikhail M. Speranskii (1772-1839),
formerly State Secretary of the Empire and more recently Governor-
General of Siberia; Admiral Nikolai Semenovich Mordvinov (1754-1845),
prominent member of the Council of State and economist; General
Aleksei Petrovich Ermolov (1772-1861), Commander-in-Chief in the Caucasus. All three had the reputation of being either liberal or opposed to
the existing regime.

3. Formation of a popular domestic guard.
4. Formation of jury courts.
5. Equalization of conscription obligations for all classes.
6. Abolition of the permanent [standing] army.
7. Establishment of the procedures for electing deputies to a Chamber of People's Representatives who will ratify the future order of government and the Constitution of the State.

Project for a Constitution by Nikita Mikhailovich Murav'ev
From *Izbrannye proizvedeniia Dekabristov*, I, 295-329.

First Draft

Introduction

The experience of all nations and of all epochs has demonstrated that autocratic power is equally ruinous for the rulers and for society: it corresponds neither to the teachings of our holy faith, nor to the principles of sane reason. One cannot admit as a principle of government one man's arbitrariness; it is impossible to accept that all rights belong to one side and all duties to the other. Blind obedience can be based only on fear and it is unworthy of both a reasonable ruler and reasonable ministers. By putting themselves above the laws, the sovereigns have forgotten that they are thereby putting themselves outside the law, outside humanity! They cannot refer to the law in cases concerning others and refuse to recognize its existence in cases concerning themselves. One of two things: either the laws are just, then why don't [the rulers] want to submit to them, or the laws are unjust, [if so] why do the rulers wish to subject others to them? All European peoples are securing laws and freedom. More than any other, the Russian people deserves to have both.

But what kind of government is appropriate to [the Russian people]? Small nations are usually prey to neighbors and do not enjoy independence. Populous nations suffer from domestic oppression, and in the hands of a despot they are often the tools of oppression and ruin for neighboring nations. The large territory and the numerous soldiers prevent some [nations] from being free; those without these inconveniences suffer from their impotence. Only a Federal or Union [form of] government has solved this problem, . . . by harmonizing the nation's expanse with its citizens' freedom.

Under the Sovereign's supervision one Legislative Assembly in the capital makes all the decisions affecting the whole state; particular decisions, affecting the [particular] regions, are left to the regional legislative assemblies, organized on the model of the one in the capital. It is in this way that the welfare of both the whole and its parts is achieved.

Second Draft

Chapter I: Of the Russian People and Government

1. Free and independent, the Russian people is not and cannot be the property of any one person or family.
2. The people is the source of *sovereign power;* to it belongs exclusively the right to make fundamental statutes for itself.

Chapter II: Of Citizens

3. Citizenship is the right to participate, according to the rules set forth in this Constitution, in the government, *indirectly*—i.e., through the election of officials or electors—*directly*—i.e., through election to any public office in the legislative, executive, or judiciary.
4. Citizens are those inhabitants of the Russian Empire who enjoy the above-mentioned rights.
5. A citizen must meet the following necessary conditions: (i) [be] no less than twenty-one years of age; (ii) [have] a permanent residence; (iii) [be] healthy of mind; (iv) [have] personal freedom; (v) punctually pay public dues; (vi) [be] in the clear with the law.
//6. and 7. deal with the status of the foreign-born.//
8. Twenty years after the promulgation of this Constitution of the Russian Empire, no one may be recognized [a] citizen who has not become literate in the Russian language.
//9. Conditions under which citizenship may be lost.//

Chapter III: Status, Personal Rights, and Obligations of Russians

10. All Russians are equal before the law.

11. Considered to be Russians are all native inhabitants of Russia and children of foreigners born in Russia who are of age and who have not made known that they do not wish to enjoy this privilege.

12. Everyone must fulfill his public obligations, obey the laws and authorities of the fatherland, and come to the defense of the homeland when required to do so by law.

13. Serfdom and slavery are abolished. The slave who touches Russian soil becomes free. No distinction is recognized between commoner and nobleman [*blagorodnyi*—well-born], for it is against our faith, according to which all men are *brothers,* well-born by divine will, all born *for the good,* and *simply men;* for all are weak and imperfect.

14. Everyone has the right freely to express his ideas and feelings and communicate them by way of print to his countrymen. Books, like all other actions, may be the object of prosecution before the courts and must be tried before a *jury.*

15. All the existing merchant and craft guilds and corporations are abolished.

16. Everyone has the right to engage in whatever trade seems most lucrative: agriculture, cattle raising, hunting, fishing, handicrafts, industry, commerce, etc.

17. Every litigation involving property exceeding the value of one pound of pure silver (twenty-five silver rubles) goes before a jury court.

18. Every criminal case is tried before a jury.

19. Anyone suspected of a crime may be put under guard by lawfully constituted authorities and in accordance with established procedures; but within twenty-four hours . . . he must be informed in writing of the cause of his detention; otherwise he is set free immediately.

20. Unless accused of a criminal offense, a prisoner is to be set free immediately if bail is put up for him.

21. No one may be punished except under provision of a law issued before the crime [was committed and] duly and legally put into effect.

22. This Constitution stipulates what officials, under what circumstances, possess the right to issue written orders for the detention of a citizen, the search of his home, the seizure of his papers, the perlustration of his letters. In the same manner the Constitution assigns responsibility for such acts.

23. The right to property, pertaining only to *things,* is sacred and intangible.

24. The landowners' lands remain their possession. The peasants' houses, gardens, all their agricultural implements, and cattle are recognized to be the property of the peasants.

25. Economic and appanage peasants are to be called *common owners,* as are free agriculturists, for the land on which they live is given to them in *common* possession and recognized as their [common] property.[2] The Appanage Administration is abolished.

26. Subsequent legislation will define the manner in which these lands will pass from *common* to *individual ownership* and the rules for repartitioning the common lands among the peasants.

27. Peasants living on leased estates[3] are also *freed,* but the land remains in the possession of the lessees for the duration of the lease.

28. The military colonies are abolished right away. Members of settled battalions and squadrons, with their families, merge into the class of common owners.

29. The division of men according to the fourteen classes of ranks is abolished.[4] Civil ranks borrowed from the Germans . . . are abolished on ground of the Russian people's old customs. . . .

30. The clergy will continue to receive their salaries. They are also freed from quartering and carting duties.

31. Nomadic tribes do not enjoy civil rights. However, they too have the right to elect township elders [*volostnoi starshina*].

32. Citizens may organize partnerships and societies without requesting permission from anyone, provided only that their actions are not unlawful.

---

[2] Economic peasants were serfs settled on former Church lands secularized by Catherine II. Appanage peasants were serfs settled on lands belonging to members of the Imperial family. Free agriculturists were private serfs freed under the Act of 1803.

[3] Estates leased by the State to individuals on favorable terms, frequently to recompense for special services or in compensation for losses.

[4] The fourteen degrees of the Table of Ranks established by Peter the Great (1722) for military, civil, and court service.

33. Every one of these societies may make its own by-laws, provided they do not conflict with this Constitution and the public laws.

34. No foreign company may have subsidiary companies or partnerships in Russia.

35. No violation of the law may be excused by reference to orders from superiors. The violator of the law is punished first, then whoever has signed the unlawful order.

36. Citizens may address their complaints and petitions to the People's Assembly (*narodnoe veche*), the Emperor, and the governing bodies of the State.

37. Underground dungeons and casemates, and in general the so-called state prisons are abolished. No one may be imprisoned anywhere except in public prisons, designated for this purpose.

38. Defendants should not be imprisoned in the same place together with convicts, nor should those sentenced for debts and petty crimes [be put] together with great criminals and monsters.

40. The present police officials are released from duty and are to be replaced on the basis of popular election.

42. No one may be disturbed in the exercise of his religion according to his conscience and feelings, as long as he does not violate the laws of nature and morality.

Chapter IV: Of Russia

43. For legislative and executive purposes all of Russia is divided into thirteen states [*derzhava*], two regions [*oblast'*], and 569 districts [*uezd*] or parishes [*povet.*] The entire population is estimated at 22,630,000 males and the representation is calculated accordingly.

Population	State	Capital
450,000	State of Bothnia	Helsingfors
1,685,000	State of Volkhov	City of St. Peter
750,000	Baltic State	Riga
2,125,000	Western State	Vil'no
2,600,000	State of the Dnieper	Smolensk
3,465,000	Black Sea State	Kiev
750,000	State of the Caucasus	Tiflis
3,500,000	Ukrainian State	Khar'kov
2,450,000	Transvolga State	Iaroslavl'
2,000,000	State of the Kama	Kazan'

Population	State	Capital
1,425,000	State of the Lower Steppe	Saratov
490,000	State of the Ob'	Tobol'sk
250,000	State of the Lena	Irkutsk
—	Moscow Region	Moscow
—	Don Region	Cherkassk

The states are subdivided into districts, districts into townships [*volost'*] of 500 to 1,500 male inhabitants. For purposes of the judiciary, the states are divided into circuits [*okrug*] equal to the present provinces [*guberniia*].

Chapter V: The Internal Organization of Townships and Districts or Parishes

44. In every district, citizens owning 500 silver rubles' worth of real estate or 1,000 silver rubles' worth of movables gather in the district capital and elect a Thousandman [*tysiatskii*] for one year. . . .

//45. Citizens owning land in common elect one elector for every 500 male inhabitants. Any common owner possessing property in his own right may participate in the elections as per article 44.//

46. A Thousandman must be at least twenty-one years old, of good conduct, and personally own real estate worth no less than 1,500 lbs. of pure silver (30,000 silver rubles) or movables worth no less than 3,000 lbs. of pure silver (60,000 silver rubles). . . .

47. The duties of the Thousandman consist in the following: (i) He assembles the citizens for elections of representatives, deputies, members of the State Dumas [i.e., assembly] etc., and presides at these [electoral] assemblies. (ii) Carries out the decisions of judges, sends out court writs, publicizes the decisions of State Governors, compiles lists of jurymen. (iii) Collects public revenues. (iv) Supervises public prisons and the execution of criminal sentences. (v) Protects officials in the exercise of their functions, submits the district's demands, speaks always in the name of the district, puts under guard disturbers of the peace—in the last-named case, everyone must obey him and assist him if called upon to do so.//(vi) Compiles two lists of inhabitants—one of those owning no less than 1,500 lbs. of silver worth of real estate or 3,000 lbs. of silver in movables, and and another of those owning no less than 250 lbs. of silver worth

of real estate or 500 lbs. of silver worth of movables. Those on the first list may be elected to various public offices.//

48. All lists must be printed and published.

51. The Thousandman must be a resident of his district. He may be reelected several times.

52. The Thousandman selects two or three assistants, depending on the size of the district, and appoints secretaries and messengers.

54. Every Thousandman, his assistant, and the Elder receive compensation at the end of the year: the Thousandman, 1,500 silver rubles; his assistant, 500 silver rubles; the Elder, 100 silver rubles.

57. The inhabitants of every township elect a township Elder for one year or more. Besides the administration of the township, his duty consists in collecting the inhabitants' declarations concerning their real and movable property, assigning them to the above-mentioned categories, and presenting these lists to the Thousandman.

//58. The Elder is under the particular jurisdiction of the Thousandman.//

Chapter VI: The People's Assembly [Narodnoe Veche]

59. The People's Assembly, consisting of the Sovereign Duma [*Verkhovnaia Duma*] and the Chamber of the People's Representatives [*Palata narodnykh predstavitelei*], is invested with all legislative power.

Chapter VII: The Chamber of Representatives, Number and Election of Representatives

60. The Chamber of Representatives is composed of members elected for two years by the citizens of the states.

61. At the time of his election, the Representative must be a resident of the state that elects him.

62. Persons who have contracted for public works cannot be representatives as long as they have not fulfilled the contracts.

//64. There is one representative for every 50,000 male inhabitants. Nomads are not counted for this purpose.//

//65. A census must be taken every ten years.//

66. Prior to the time [of the first census] the number of representatives is set at 450. Electoral assemblies are held every two years on the last Tuesday of September. . . .

//70. The apportionment of representatives among the districts and parishes is made by the government authorities of every state.//

72. The Chamber of Representatives elects its own president; it alone has the right to impeach the *dignitaries* of the *Empire*.

Chapter VIII: The Sovereign Duma

73. The Sovereign Duma is composed of three citizens from every state, two from the Moscow Region, and one from the Don Region, forty-two members altogether. Members of the Sovereign Duma are elected by the governing institutions of the states and regions, i.e., by the Chambers of Delegates [*Palata vybornykh*] and State Dumas [*Derzhavnaia Duma*] together.

//74. The members of the Sovereign Duma are renewed by thirds every two years; vacancies are filled on a temporary basis by the executive of the states.//

//75. Conditions of eligibility to the Sovereign Duma: thirty years old, citizen for at least nine years, residence in the state, property worth 1,500 lbs. of silver in real estate or 3,000 lbs. of silver in movables.//

//76. The Sovereign Duma elects its own president and officers.//

//77. The Sovereign Duma tries imperial government dignitaries impeached by the Chamber of Representatives. Sentencing [is] only on the basis of a two-thirds majority. Together with the Emperor, the Sovereign Duma participates in concluding peace and in appointing judges to superior courts, commanders-in-chief of naval and army forces, commanders of army corps and naval squadrons; the Duma's decision in these matters must be by a two-thirds majority.//

Chapter IX: Power and Privilege of the People's Assembly, and the Making of Laws

78. The People's Assembly meets at least once a year. Its sessions open on the first Tuesday of December (unless changed by law).

79. Each Chamber decides on the rights and credentials of its members. In both, a majority is sufficient for decision; but one-fourth of the membership may adjourn meetings from day to day until the arrival of other members and force attendance by means of whatever fines both Chambers may establish.

80. Each Chamber may punish its members for unbecoming behavior and in case of crime—*but never for an opinion;* it may expel a member by a two-thirds majority.

81. The sessions of both Chambers are public. But at the Emperor's suggestion, both Chambers may deliberate behind closed doors. . . . The same occurs in the Chamber of Representatives at the demand of five members. Women, and minors under seventeen years, are not admitted to the sessions of either Chamber.

82. Each Chamber keeps minutes and publishes them periodically, except what has been decided to keep secret. . . .

//83. Members receive compensation from the Treasury of the State on the basis of days of attendance.//

//84. Members have immunity from arrest except for treason.//

85. No official in public service may be a member of either Chamber as long as he retains his official position.

86. Neither a member of the Duma nor a Representative may be appointed to a government office during the entire term for which he has been elected. . . .

87. The Chamber of Representatives first debates any new tax or levy of conscripts. But the Duma may make amendments as in every other bill. The Duma's changes in the tax bill become effective only if the Chamber agrees to them.

88. Each bill must have three readings in every Chamber; three days at least must elapse after each reading. After each reading there is debate. After the second reading the bill is printed and distributed among all members present.

89. To receive force of law, each bill passed by the Duma and Chamber of Representatives must be submitted to the Emperor. If the Emperor approves, he signs the bill; if he disapproves he sends it back with his comments to the Chamber where it had been initiated. The Chamber enters into its minutes all the Emperor's comments and reopens the debate. If after this second debate two-thirds of the members remain in favor of the bill it goes with the

Emperor's comments to the other Chamber, where it is debated anew, and if approved by *majority* vote, it becomes law. . . .

90. A bill not returned by the Emperor within ten days (exclusive of Sundays) becomes law. If in the meantime the People's Assembly adjourns, the bill does not become law. . . . Every law, proclamation, etc., requiring the assent of both Chambers must be submitted for approval to the Emperor; his rejection can be overruled by a two-thirds vote in each Chamber. . . .

92. The People's Assembly has the power to make and abrogate laws pertaining to the judiciary and the executive, i.e.: (i) Draft a civil, criminal, commercial, and military code for Russia; set up institutions of public welfare, establish judicial procedures, and provide for the internal organization of administrative offices. (ii) In case of invasion or rebellion it proclaims the laws that put a particular region on war footing and under martial law. (iii) Publish laws of amnesty. (iv) Dissolve the government assemblies of the states if they exceed their rights, and order . . . new elections. (v) Declare war. (vi) Supervise administration of military forces, fortresses, etc. . . . (vii) Taxes, loans, audits of expenditures, pensions, salaries, all collections and expenditures—in short, [it legislates] on all financial matters; it cannot, however, approve budgets for a period exceeding two years. (viii) [It is concerned] with all government measures regarding industry, the national economy, the establishment of postal service, the maintenance of public land and waterways, the creation of new ones, the establishment of banks, etc. (ix) It protects sciences and the useful arts; it grants authors and inventors the exclusive rights to [derive] benefits from their writings and inventions. (x) Set the rules for rewarding officials, the rules of the civil service in all branches, regulations for the statistical accounts of all branches of government. (xi) Receive reports of ministers; in the case of physical or mental illness of the Emperor, his death or abdication, it either establishes a regency or proclaims the heir Emperor. (xii) Elect the governors of the states.

93. The People's Assembly has neither the power to make new *constitutional laws* nor abrogate existing ones; it cannot legislate on anything not specifically provided in its enumerated powers.

94. The People's Assembly, composed of men elected by the Russian people and representing it, assumes the character of Majesty.

95. The People's Assembly establishes common taxes and expenditures, leaving particular ones to the State Assemblies. . . .

97. From time to time, the People's Assembly publishes for the information of the whole nation a detailed account of all public receipts and expenditures. No monies are paid by the Russian Treasury, except as provided by law confirmed by the People's Assembly. (i) The right to change the Constitution or to elect another dynasty to the throne belongs to the People's States' Congresses (*sobor*) and not the People's Assembly.

98. The People's Assembly has the right neither to establish nor to prohibit any denomination or sect. The citizen's faith, conscience, and opinions are not subject to the power of the People's Assembly. . . . The People's Assembly may not violate freedom of speech and press.

99. The People's Assembly neither debates nor votes in the presence of the Emperor. In response to the Emperor's speech, the presidents of both Chambers must reply that the People's Assembly will take under consideration his proposals.

100. The People's Assembly has the right to take over private property for public use in return for just compensation; but a law must be passed to this effect, in advance, according to regular procedure. . . .

Chapter X: The Supreme Executive Power

    SECTION 1: THE EMPEROR
    SECTION 2: THE TEMPORARY REGENT
    SECTION 3: THE HEADS OF DEPARTMENTS (*prikaz*)

101. The Emperor is the supreme official of the Russian government. His rights and privileges are as follows: (i) His power is hereditary in direct line from father to son, but from the father-in-law it passes to the son-in-law. (ii) In his person he combines all executive power. (iii) He has the right to stop [the actions] of the legislative branch and compel it to reconsider the bill. (iv) He is commander-in-chief of the armed forces on land and sea. (v) He is the supreme head of any militia unit in active duty for the Empire. (vi) He may demand the written opinion of the head official of any executive department concerning any problem related to his duties. (vii) He negotiates with foreign powers and concludes peace treaties

with the advice and consent of two-thirds of the voting members of the Supreme Duma; a treaty concluded in this manner becomes a sovereign law [i.e., the law of the land].//(viii) He appoints ambassadors and high officials.//(ix) He may not include in the treaties any article that would violate the rights and property of citizens inside the fatherland. Without consent of the People's Assembly he may not include any stipulation to attack some country and he may not relinquish any territory belonging to Russia. (x) He appoints judges to Superior Courts with the advice and consent of the Sovereign Duma. (xii) He appoints the heads of all branches of the government and of all Departments (*prikaz*) such as: Head of the Treasury Department (Minister of Finance), Head of the Department for Land Forces (Minister of War), Head of the Department for Naval Forces (Minister of the Navy), Head of the Department of Foreign Relations.//(xiii) At every session of both Chambers he provides the People's Assembly with information on conditions in Russia.//(xiv) He may convoke the two Chambers and, in case of [treaty] negotiations or [state] trials, the Sovereign Duma. (xv) In case of rebellion, he may not use military forces inside Russia without submitting the proposal to the People's Assembly, which must immediately, through an investigation, satisfy itself of the necessity of a state of siege. (xvii) If the two Chambers cannot agree on a date of adjournment, the Emperor may adjourn them, but for no longer than three months. (xviii) He receives ambassadors and accredited plenipotentiaries of foreign powers. (xix) He supervises the strict application of public laws. (xx) He issues commissions to all officials of the Empire. (xxi) He has the title of "His Imperial Majesty"; no other title is recognized. . . . (xxii) The People's Assembly determines the formal procedure by which a new Emperor assumes his office. (xxiii) Upon his accession, the Emperor takes the following oath in the People's Assembly: "I solemnly swear that I will faithfully carry out the duties of a Russian Emperor and with all my might preserve and defend this Constitution of Russia."

//102. The Emperor's particular income is abolished. He receives two million silver rubles yearly for which he need not render account. . . .//

103. Members of the Imperial family are not distinguished from private persons; they are subject to the same rules and the same acts of the government as all others and enjoy no special rights or privileges.

//104. Court officials receive no salaries from public funds. They may receive compensation from the Emperor's own civil list of eight millions. Courtiers lose their rights as citizens, i.e., they may not elect or be elected, or appointed to official posts while they are in the service of one person.//

//105. The ruler of the Empire may not leave the Empire without creating serious difficulties.//

106. The Emperor's departure from the Empire is considered tantamount to his leaving it and abdicating his imperial calling; in such a case the People's Assembly immediately proclaims the heir Emperor.

//107. Cases of regency.//

//108. Temporary regency under the President of the Sovereign Duma when a new Emperor is not of age.//

//111. Women are excluded from the throne and do not transmit any rights to it. When a line ends, the people will determine the form of government or elect another dynasty.//

//112. The Emperor signs no papers, except treaties, commissions, reports on the state of the Empire, bills. All other official papers are signed by the heads of executive departments.//

//113–114. Concerning the responsibility of all officials. The Emperor can do no wrong. If he commits a crime he is adjudged to have been mentally ill and a regency is appointed.//

Chapter XI: Domestic Authorities and Governors of States

115. The government of every state consists of three separate powers, mutually independent yet working toward the same end, namely, the governing, executive, and judiciary powers.

Chapter XII: The Governing Power of States

116. The governing power of every state is entrusted to a Governing Assembly (*pravitel'stvuiushchee sobranie*) consisting of a Chamber of Delegates (*palata vybornykh*) and the Duma. The Governing Assembly meets in the capital city of each state.

SECTION 1: THE CHAMBER OF DELEGATES

//117. (i) Members are elected for one year. (ii) The conditions for election are the same as in article 5, paragraph 1. (iii) There is

one Delegate for every 10,000 male inhabitants. (iv) One-quarter of
the state Duma is renewed every year.//

SECTION 2: THE STATE DUMA

//118. (i) Members [are] elected for four years by the same electors as for the Delegates. (ii) Members must be thirty years old, have
been citizens for nine years, have 750 lbs. of silver worth of real
estate or 1,500 lbs. of silver worth of movables. (iii) The Duma membership is about one-third that of the Chamber of Delegates.//

SECTION 3: THE INTERNAL ORGANIZATION AND POWERS
OF THE GOVERNING ASSEMBLY

//119. (i) In session once a year; duration of session depends
on business. (ii) Elects own officers; members are compensated for
each day in session. (iii) Members may be reelected. (iv) No official
may be a member. Legislative initiative belongs to both Chambers
and to the Governor, except that all tax bills go first to the Chamber
of Delegates. The state Duma tries officials impeached by the Chamber of Delegates. (v) Debates are public, unless executive session
is requested by one-third of members. (vi) Members are immune
from arrest, except in cases of treason, violation of public order, and
heinous crime. (vii) Each Chamber may reject decision of the other.
Governor may refuse to sign bill, returning it to the Chamber where
it originated within ten days. (viii) The Governor's objections are
overridden in the same way as those of the Emperor in the People's
Assembly. (ix) The Governing Assembly in every state has the following rights: make laws for the internal administration of the
state; make new administrative subdivisions for the area; establish
electoral centers; raise taxes for expenditures necessary to the administration and welfare of the state (i.e., means of transportation,
justice, salaries, etc.)—taxes to cover national needs (defense, postal
service, etc.) are established by the People's Assembly; set up necessary public institutions like schools; maintain means of transportation; petition the People's Assembly to call a People's Convention
to amend the Constitution; it may not meet in towns occupied by
the enemy or by rebels.//

Chapter XIII: The Executive Power in the States

120. The executive power in every state is entrusted to a state
Governor [*derzhavnyi pravitel'*], his Lieutenant, and a Council.

//Must be thirty years old, have been citizen for nine years, own 1,500 lbs. of silver worth of real estate or 3,000 lbs. of silver worth of movables.//

121. Every three years the People's Assembly elects the Governors from among a list of candidates submitted by the Governing Assemblies. These elections are made by the two Chambers of the People's Assembly sitting together and are confirmed by the Emperor.

122. The rights and duties of the Governor are as follows: //(i) He confirms laws passed by the Governing Assembly or returns them for renewed consideration. (ii-iii) Adjourns Governing Assemblies, but for no more than ninety days. (iv) He closes the yearly session of the Governing Assembly. (v) Orders the Governing Assembly to meet in another town if the capital is threatened by epidemic disease or other danger. (vi) He is commander-in-chief of his state's militia, but cannot send it beyond the boundaries of the state without the consent of the Governing Assembly. He may not use the militia against the population in case of rebellion before the Governing Assembly declares martial law. (vii) On recommendation of his Council, he appoints: the State Keeper of the Laws, State Judges, and other officials on the first list. (viii) He receives a salary of 10,000 rubles yearly.//

123. Upon completion of his term, a Governor may be appointed for a second time only after four years have elapsed; the same applies to the Lieutenant [Governor] and Councilors.

124. Every three years, on the last Tuesday of November, both Chambers assemble to elect together the Lieutenant and Councilors. A majority of two-thirds of members present is required for election.

125. To be a Lieutenant or Councilor a candidate must meet the same qualifications as the Governor.

126. Depending on the size of the state, the number of Councilors is nine, seven, or five.//List of apportionment per state.//

127. Five out of nine, four out of seven, three out of five Councilors must always be present.

//128. Minutes of decisions and opinions of the Council are kept and must be presented to the Chambers of the Assembly upon request.//

129. A dissenting Councilor may demand that his opinion be entered in full in the minutes. The Council participates in all decisions and actions of the Governor.

130. In case the voices are split equally, the opinion of the

Governor is decisive.//Councilors receive the same compensation as the members of the Duma.//

131. One-third of the Council is renewed every year. . . .

132. The Lieutenant Governor has the following rights: (i) Presides in the Council during lengthy absences of the Governor, but has no voice. In the absence of the Governor, therefore, the Council holds all executive power. (ii) In case of vacancy of the governorship through illness, death, or other cause, the Lieutenant takes his place and assumes all his powers. (iii) Receives a yearly compensation of 5,000 silver rubles.

133. State Secretary, State Treasurer, State Collector of Customs. All three are elected every three years by both Chambers sitting together.

134. The Governor, the Lieutenant Governor, the Keeper of the Laws, the Secretary, the Treasurer, and all civil officials may be deprived of their functions if, after impeachment by the Chamber of Delegates, they will be convicted by the Duma for treason, misappropriation of public funds, other crimes or vicious behavior.

V

The Southern Society

The Southern Society had been organized as a branch of the original Decembrist group centered in St. Petersburg. Its main leader was Colonel Pavel Pestel', whose powerful personality could not accept a secondary role and whose domineering character made him a dictatorial leader par excellence. The ranks of the Southern Society were swollen by former officers of the Semenovskii Guard regiment who had been transferred to line regiments after the Semenovskii mutiny in 1820. Under the influence of Pestel', many of these former Guard officers became the most radical spokesmen of the Decembrist movement. Thus Sergei Ivanovich Murav'ev-Apostol wrote the "Catechism" and the "Proclamation" in such a way as to enlist the active participation and loyalty of the ordinary soldiers (something which the members of the Northern Society shied from doing even on December 14). He also led the abortive mutiny in Chernigov, in the vain hope of linking forces with what he believed to be the successful rebellion in St. Petersburg.

But in a sense the Southern Society was the creation of Pestel'. It was he who organized it, enrolled its most important members, and wrote its program, which also was a draft constitution for Russia—the so-called Russian Law. Although Pestel' worked on it for several years, it remained uncompleted; the chapters dealing with the political organization, for example, are still in draft form. If

Murav'ev's project was inspired by the Constitution of the United States, Pestel' 's Russian Law was directly influenced by the radical French political writers of the eighteenth century and the policies of the Jacobins. His Russia was to be a centralized, unitary state, "one and indivisible," like revolutionary France. Curiously enough, although Murav'ev envisaged a federal system, he paid no attention to the fact that Russia was a multinational empire. Pestel', on the other hand (perhaps because he was the son of a Governor-General of Siberia of German ancestry, had been educated in Germany, and had spent many years of his army career in the Ukraine), was acutely aware of the non-Russian nationalities. But his solution was to abolish distinctive nationalities by the merging of all inhabitants of Russia into one single culture. In spite of the great debt he owed to French thought, Pestel' tried to give his program a Russian form by using (or devising) old-fashioned historical terms for his categories and institutions. It should also be noted that Pestel' 's political radicalism was not matched by any radicalism in social and economic matters; in this respect he advocated moderate economic liberalism.

Orthodox Catechism by Sergei Ivanovich Murav'ev-Apostol
From *Vosstanie Dekabristov,* IV (1927), 254-55.

In the Name of the Father and the Son and the Holy Ghost.
Question. For what purpose did God create man?
Answer. So that he would believe in Him, be free and happy.
Q. What does it mean to believe in God?
A. Our God, Jesus Christ, who descended to earth for our Salvation has left us His Holy Gospel. To believe in God means to follow in everything the true meaning of the laws inscribed in it.
Q. What does it mean to be free and happy?
A. Without freedom there is no happiness. The Apostle Paul says: "You have been bought at the price of blood, you shall not be slaves of man." [1]

---

[1] Slight misquoting of I Cor. 7:23: "You are bought with a price; be not ye the servants of men."

Q. Why are the Russian people and army unhappy?

A. Because the Tsars[2] robbed them of freedom.

Q. Consequently the Tsars are acting against God's will?

A. Yes, of course, our God has said: "But he that is greatest among you shall be your servant" [Matt. 23:11], while the Tsars only tyrannize the people.

Q. Should one obey Tsars when they act against God's will?

A. No. Christ has said, you cannot serve God and Mammon [Matt. 6:24]; the Russian people and the Russian army suffer because they submit to Tsars.

Q. What does our Holy Writ command the Russian people and army to do?

A. To repent of their long servility and, rising against tyranny and lawlessness, to swear: let there be one Tsar for all, Jesus Christ in Heaven and on earth.

Q. What can prevent this sacred deed?

A. Nothing. Those who oppose this sacred deed are traitors, apostates, who have sold their soul to lawlessness; and woe to them, hypocrites, for God's terrible punishment will be theirs in this world and in the other.

Q. In what manner are we to rise with a pure heart?

A. Take up arms and bravely follow those who speak up in the name of the Lord, remembering the words of our Saviour: "Blessed are they which do hunger and thirst after righteousness, for they shall be filled" [Matt. 5:6], and after destroying impiety and lawlessness of tyranny, reestablish a government based on God's law.

Q. What government accords with God's law?

A. One in which there are no Tsars. God has created us all equal and descending on earth he chose his Apostles from among the common people and not from among the nobles and kings.

Q. Consequently, God does not like Tsars?

A. No. They have been cursed by Him as oppressors of the

---

[2] Throughout this text, the Russian word Tsar is used to denote the Russian monarchs and kings in both the generic and Biblical meaning of ruler. Both Tsar and King have been used, depending on the context, to translate the single Russian term, in order not to lose the specific allusion to Russian circumstances.

people. But God loves man. Let anyone who wants to know of God's judgment of kings read the Book of Kings, chapter 8: "Then all the elders of Israel gathered themselves together and came to Samuel . . . and said unto him . . . now make us a king to judge us. . . . But the thing displeased Samuel. . . . And Samuel prayed unto the Lord. And the Lord said unto Samuel: Hearken unto the voice of the people in all that they say unto thee, for they have not rejected thee, but they have rejected me, that I should not reign over them . . . and show them the manner of the king. . . . And Samuel told all the words of the Lord unto the people that asked of him a king. And he said, This will be the manner of the king that shall reign over you: He will take your sons . . . and he will take your daughters . . . and he will take the tenth of your seed . . . and ye shall be his servants. And ye shall cry out in that day because of your king which ye shall have chosen you; and the Lord will not hear you in that day." [3] And thus the election of kings is against the will of God, for Jesus Christ should be our only King.

Q. Consequently, the oath to the Tsar is contrary to God?

A. Yes. It is contrary to God. Tsars command the people to swear forced oaths for their destruction and call the Name of the Lord in vain. But our Saviour Jesus Christ has said: "But I say unto you, swear not at all" [Matt. 5:34], and thus any oath to a man is contrary to God, for it belongs to Him alone.

Q. Why are the Tsars mentioned in church?

A. Because of the Tsars' own impious orders for the deception of the people, and the hourly repetition of the Tsar's name befouls the divine service in spite of the Saviour's command: "But when ye pray, use not vain repetitions, as the heathen do" [Matt. 6:7].

Q. What should the Christ-loving Russian army do then?

A. For the liberation of their suffering families and country, and for the accomplishment of the Holy Christian Writ [they should]: After offering a warm and hope-filled prayer to God, Who fights for truth and clearly protects those who have strong faith in Him, rise all together against tyranny and reestablish faith and liberty in Russia.

---

[3] I Sam. 8:5-18. In the Russian Scriptures this book is also called Book of Kings.

And on him who stays behind, as on Judas the Traitor, let there be a curse and anathema.

AMEN

Proclamation of the Southern Society
by Sergei Ivanovich Murav'ev-Apostol
From *Vosstanie Dekabristov*, IV (1927), 256.

God has taken pity on Russia. He has sent death to our tyrant. Christ has said: "Be no man's slaves, you who have been redeemed by my blood." [4] The world has not hearkened to His holy command and has fallen into an abyss of misery. But our sufferings have moved the Almighty—today He sends you freedom and salvation.

Brethren, let us repent of our long-lasting servility and let us swear that we shall have but one Tsar, Jesus Christ, in Heaven and on earth.

All the miseries of the Russian people have come from autocratic government. It has fallen. By the death of the tyrant God has manifested His will that we cast off the fetters of slavery contrary to Christian law. From now on Russia is free. But as true sons of the Church we shall not perpetrate any outrages and without internecine strife we shall establish a popular government based on God's law that says, "Let the first among you serve you."

The Russian army is approaching to reestablish a popular government derived from Christian principles, based on Holy Writ. No crimes will be committed. And thus, let our pious people remain at peace and in order, and implore the Almighty for the speedy conclusion of our sacred deed. Let the servants of the altar, until now left in poverty and neglect by our impious tyrant, pray God for us, as we restore the Lord's temples to all their splendor.

---

[4] See note 1.

The Russian Law[5] by Pavel Ivanovich Pestel'
From *Vosstanie Dekabristov*, VIII (1958), 113-68, 169-209.

Second Draft

Introduction

BASIC CONCEPTS

¶*1. Every society has its goal and selects means to attain it.*

Every association of several persons for the *attainment of some goal* is called a *society*. The stimulus for such an association or goal is usually the satisfaction of *common* needs, which, as they derive from the common and identical characteristics of man, are the same for all men. From this follows that members of *any* society may reach unanimous agreement on the *goal*. But when they turn to the action or *means* by which the goal is to be reached, there must arise among them violent disputes and endless disagreements, because the *selection of means* does not depend so much on the common traits of human nature as on the peculiar character and personal qualities of each person in particular. The character and personal qualities of people are so varied that if everyone were to remain set in his own opinion, not listening to the opinions of others, it would be impossible to select the means for reaching the assigned goal, and still less [possible] to devise the method and proceed to action. In such a case nothing remains but to destroy the society prior to any action. But if the members do not wish to destroy society, every one of them must give up some of his own opinions and ideas to create a *single* opinion on whose basis the means for action could be selected.

---

[5] The full title of the manuscript is: "Russian Law, or Prescriptive Political Charter of the Great Russian Nation, to serve as Precept for the Improvement of the Political Organization of Russia and containing a Just Instruction for the People as well as for the Provisional Supreme Administration."

¶2. *Division of members of society into those who command and those who obey.*

But who will propose such a *definitive* opinion, who will select the means, who will determine the methods, who will organize action? All these difficulties can be resolved in two ways: In the *first* case, the moral superiority of one or several members reconciles the various difficulties and carries with it the other [members of society] on the strength of its excellence, sometimes aided by other external circumstances. In the *second* case, the members of society entrust one or several among them with the task of selecting the means, putting at their disposal the right to decide on common action. In either case members of society are divided into those who command and those who obey. This distinction is unavoidable, for it is derived from human nature, and consequently exists, and should exist, everywhere. This natural division is the foundation for the difference in rights and duties of each.

¶3. *Division of the state into the government and the people.*

All that has been said here of societies in general pertains in equal measure to *civil societies,* which, after they have been established and organized, receive the name of *state.* Like any other, *civil society* has its goal and must select means to attain it. The goal consists in the *welfare*[6] *of society in general and of each one of its members in particular.* Everyone agrees on this *goal.* To attain it, *means* or actions are necessary. These means are divided into general and particular ones. *General* actions are those which affect all of society and, therefore, are carried out in the name of society as a whole. *Particular* [actions] consist of the occupation and activity of every member in particular. The selection of the *means* for the attainment of the said goal, and action in accordance with this selection, bring about the division of members of civil society into *those who command and those who obey.* Action in the name of society as a whole is the duty of the former, action in the name of private members is left to the latter. When a civil society acquires

---

* Pestel' uses the word *blagodenstvie,* which may also be translated as happiness. Both welfare and happiness have been used as a translation of *blagodenstvie* throughout the Russian Law.

the name of *state,* then those who command are called *government* and those who obey are called *people.* From this it follows that the main and original component parts of every state are: the *government* and the *people.*

¶*4. Mutual relationships between government and people.*

The government has the *duty* to organize common action and to select the best means for securing the welfare of all and each in the state; for this reason it has the *right* to demand obedience from the people. The people, on the other hand, have the *duty* to obey the government, but in return they have the *right* to demand that the government strive without fail for both general and particular happiness and command only what truly leads to this goal and without which the goal would not be reached. The existence of any government can be based only on this balance of mutual obligations and rights. That is why when a government loses this balance, its natural and healthy condition is changed into one of violence and disease. The major aim of this Russian Law, and the basic duty of every legislator, is to rest this balance on firm foundations.

¶*5. Every right must be based on a prior obligation.*

Obligations have been mentioned here before *rights* because a right is only the consequence of an obligation and exists solely on the basis of a preexistent duty. The original obligation of man, which serves as the source and cause of all other obligations, is the preservation of his existence. Besides natural reason, this is proven by the words in the Scriptures which contain the whole Christian law: "Love God" and "Love thy neighbor as thyself"; words which imply love of oneself as the necessary condition of human nature; it is a natural law, and consequently our duty. From this obligation stems the right to use the fruits and other products of nature as foodstuffs. Man has this right only because he has the duty to preserve his existence. In exactly the same way a right—whatever it be—can exist and be recognized as valid only when it is necessary for the fulfillment of the obligation that precedes it, and on which it . . . is based. A right without a prior obligation is nothing, means nothing, and is to be considered as mere violence and tyranny.

¶6. Basic notions of the state's welfare and of the obligations connected with it.

In a state, therefore, the main concern is to have a conception of every obligation from which derives a corresponding right. Obligations in the state derive from the goals of the state. The goal of the state's organization must be the welfare of each and all. And, therefore, everything that leads to welfare is an obligation. But inasmuch as the conceptions of welfare are quite varied, some basic or fundamental rules must be established. The obligations that God imposes on man through faith are the first and the most essential. They connect the spiritual world with the natural, life on this earth with life eternal—and all government statutes, therefore, must be related to and in accord with man's obligations toward faith and the All Highest Maker of Worlds. This first order of obligations pertains to the spiritual domain and is known to us from Holy Writ. The second order of obligations pertains to the world of nature, and is known to us from the laws of nature and natural needs. God, Creator of the Universe, is also the creator of the laws of nature, or natural needs. These laws are deeply engraved in our hearts. Every man is subject to them, no one has the power to destroy them; and for this reason government statutes should be as much in accord with the immutable laws of nature as with the sacred laws of faith. Finally, a third order of obligations arises out of the formation of civil societies or states. With respect to it the first rule is that every effort in the state to secure its welfare must accord with the spiritual and natural laws. The second rule: all government statutes must aim exclusively at the welfare of civil society, and every act contrary or harmful to it must be considered a crime. The third rule: the common weal must be esteemed more important than private happiness, and in case of conflict the former takes precedence. The fourth rule: the common weal must be seen as the welfare of the totality of the people; from this follows that the state organization's true aim must necessarily be: the greatest possible happiness of the greatest number of people in the state. That is why the benefit of one or a part must always yield to the benefit of all, the whole being defined as the totality or mass of the people. Lastly, the fifth rule states that the private individual, in making efforts to secure his happiness, must not step outside his field of action and encroach upon another's. That is, the happiness of one man should not bring harm, and still less, destruction, to another. No sooner will all the actions of the government and of private individuals be based on these rules, than the state will doubtlessly enjoy all the happiness possible. All laws and government statutes must definitely be in complete agreement with these rules.

¶7. *The basic notion regarding the people and its significance.*

It has been made clear above that the state consists of the government and the people. The people is the sum total of all those who, belonging to the same state, constitute the civil society whose aim it is to [make] possible the happiness of each and all. According to the immutable law of civil society every state is composed of the people and the government; consequently the people are not the government, and each has its own particular obligations and rights. The government, however, exists only for the good of the people and it has no other ground for its existence and organization than the people's good. Whereas the people exists for its own good and to carry out the will of the Almighty who has called men to this earth to glorify His Name, be virtuous and happy. This divine law applies equally to all men, and consequently all have an equal right to its implementation. And that is the reason why the Russian people is not the possession or the property of some one person or family; on the contrary, the government is the property of the people and it has been established for the good of the people, and not the people for the good of the government.

¶8. *Basic notions concerning the government and its division into sovereign power and state administration.*

The government is the sum total of all persons engaged in managing public affairs. It has the obligation of procuring happiness for the people and for this reason it has the right to govern the state so as to attain this set goal. Having this right, it should also possess the corresponding power, so that it may fulfill this obligation and actually [exercise] this right. This power, by means of which the government carries out its obligations, makes use of its right, and attains the set goal, is the *sovereign power* [*verkhovnaia vlast'*]. . . . From the sovereign power are derived particular powers which encompass the government's entire purpose. That is why the particular authorities must depend entirely on the sovereign power and act along the lines set by it. The sum total of all these particular or special authorities constitutes the *state administration,* which may also be called the *officialdom [chinonachal'stvo]*. From this it follows that the government cannot fulfill its obligations and secure the state's welfare if it does not possess an authority commensurate with the importance and extent of civil society's goal, and if this authority's action does not reach into all fields throughout the state and at the same time does not have many subordinate authorities which are concerned with only particular fields or parts thereof. The general authority is called sovereign power and the sum total of particular authorities, the state administration or officialdom. For this reason any government is divided into the sovereign power and the state administration or officialdom.

¶9. *The division of the state's welfare into security and prosperity.*

A *state's welfare* consists of two main objects: *security* and *prosperity*. The distinguishing and principal characteristic of security is *safeguard,* while that of prosperity is *acquisition*. Security must be the first aim of the government because it may be attained only by the common action of united forces and wills: it is precisely this combination which is present in the government, and it corresponds to the *original* duty of man consisting in the preservation of his existence. In addition, without security there can be no prosperity; therefore, it serves as the foundation to the edifice of government. Prosperity must be the *second* aim of government, for there are so many notions of it that it must be left to every particular member of civil society to secure it; and the government's participation in this respect must be limited to giving protection and eliminating those obstacles which exceed the strength and capacities of private persons. This is the more true since private individuals can gain prosperity by their own means, but cannot safeguard their security by private means.

¶10. *Necessity of transforming Russia and of issuing new laws.*

Such are the essential fundamental concepts on which the existence, life, and organization of any well-ordered state should be based: that it be under the power and rule of political laws and not

under a ruler's personal caprice, and that the state provide for the
possible happiness of each and all [instead of] governing abusively
all for the advantage of one or several [individuals]. Everything
departing from these rules, and still more [everything] contradicting
them, is an abuse of power, a destruction of rights . . . that brings
about blame and results in disaster. Applying these unchangeable
and immutable fundamental principles to Russia, one clearly sees
that these fundamental principles themselves necessarily demand
the transformation of Russia's present political order and its re-
placement by an organization based only on precise and just laws,
leaving nothing to personal arbitrariness and absolutely guaranteeing to the Russian people its existence as an organized civil society
that is not, and never would be, [anyone's] possession or property.
From this there follow two principal needs for Russia: the first
consists in a complete transformation of the order of government
and the second in the issuance of a complete new Code or collection
of laws that will preserve everything useful and destroy all that is
harmful.

¶*11. Of the necessity of a Russian Law and a Provisional*
Supreme Administration.

This double goal cannot be successfully attained except through
the establishment of a Provisional Supreme Administration and the
publication of a Russian Law for the information of all. The reasons
are as follows: The prospective new order, because of the state's
size and of the great number of laws and fields subject to transformation, cannot be introduced at once. Many measures of a preparatory or transitional character are necessary to this end and they
should be introduced gradually, so as not to subject the state to
disorders, turmoil, and transformations which instead of improving
would ruin it. All the events that have taken place in Europe over
the last half century show that peoples who have been fired by the
expectation that sudden measures were feasible and have rejected
gradual government reform have been cast into dreadful miseries
and subjected anew to the yoke of despotism and lawlessness. This
proves the necessity of initiating the transformation of the government by means of gradual steps. Who can be entrusted with this
important matter but the Provisional Supreme Administration? The
previous supreme power has sufficiently proven its enmity toward

the Russian people; and a representative Congress (*sobor*) cannot be convened, for there exists as yet no foundation for a supreme representative system in Russia. But inasmuch as Russia must have a pledge that the Provisional Supreme Administration will act exclusively for the good of Russia and the improvement of its condition . . . in all fields and respects, it is necessary to issue a Russian Law in the form of instructions to the Supreme Administration. On the other hand, the drafting of a Code or a complete compendium of laws is a vast and difficult undertaking requiring much time and much reflection if it is to bring the [various] laws into harmony and accord; that is why it cannot be issued at once and now. The Code of the state, moreover, ought to contain only the precise or positive laws and statutes that will establish the *future* order of government, and consequently it should not include [any of the following]: (1) memories of the present order, for [this] will have ceased to exist; (2) an exposition of the transitional and preparatory measures by means of which the present order will be replaced by the prospective new one, for preparatory and transitional measures are provisional actions; finally, (3) clarification of basic theoretical considerations and principles on which the edifice of government is to be erected, for theoretic speculations should not be included among positive laws or in the Code. But as these three matters are of vital importance and Russia from the very inception of its rebirth and transformation must know them, there is proven need for a Russian Law setting forth the basic principles and foundations of this transformation, and at the same time containing regulations for the whole state as well as for its members and parts.

¶*12. Definition, aim, and action of the Russian Law.*

The Russian law, therefore, is the Supreme All Russian Charter setting forth all the changes to be made in the state, all the things and rules subject to abrogation and elimination, and lastly, the basic rules and fundamental principles which are to serve as immutable guidelines in establishing the new order of government and in drafting the new Constitution. It contains . . . some of the most important positive laws and statutes pertaining to the future order of things, the enumeration of the principal transitional measures, and also an explanation of the basic principles, fundamental causes, and principal considerations sanctioning the proposed order of govern-

ment for Russia. In this manner the Russian Law is an instruction
or prescription for the actions of the Provisional Supreme Administration and at the same time a proclamation to the people [inform-
ing them] of what they have been freed and what they may still
expect. It states the obligations imposed on the Provisional Supreme
Administration and serves as a pledge to Russia that the Provisional
Supreme Administration will act exclusively for the good of the
fatherland. The absence of such a charter has brought most dreadful calamities and internecine strife to many states, because their
governments were always able to act arbitrarily, motivated by personal passions and private interests, without clear and complete
instructions to guide them. And in the meantime the people, never
knowing what was done for them, never aware of the goal to which
the government's actions were directed, were agitated by numerous
fears and passions which brought them . . . to civil strife. By the
very fact of its existence the Russian Law forestalls this evil and
positively initiates the active transformation of the state by defining
everything and issuing fundamental rules for all matters. The
Provisional Supreme Administration—in all branches and at all
levels of government—as well as the entire people—all its members
or citizens—must, therefore, conform to the Russian Law. The
Provisional Supreme Administration must introduce by gradual
measures the new order of government defined in the Russian Law,
while the people not only must not resist their introduction but, on
the contrary, must zealously and with all their might assist the Provisional Supreme Administration, not letting undue impatience
harm the success of the nation's regeneration and the state's transformation.

¶13. *Division of the Russian Law into chapters.*

To this purpose the Russian Law is divided into ten chapters.

The first discusses the frontiers of the state and its territorial
divisions: it shows where the Russian state is situated.

The second treats of the people with respect to the various
races living within the Russian state.

The third chapter discusses the nation with respect to the
various estates in the Russian state.

The fourth chapter treats of the nation with respect to its
planned political or social order.

The fifth treats of the nation with respect to its planned civil or private order.

The sixth discusses the government in relation to the organization and establishment of the Sovereign Power.

The seventh discusses the government in relation to the organization and establishment of the state administration.

The eighth treats of the government with respect to the establishment of security within the state.

The ninth treats of the government with respect to the establishment of prosperity in the state.

The tenth contains an instruction for the drafting of a state Code that would be a complete compendium of all laws and statutes. Moreover, the Russian Law contains an *Introduction* setting forth the general notions on which any government system is based and in guise of *conclusion* a brief summary of the main decisions and statutes introduced by the Russian law. . . .

Chapter I: Of the State's Territory

¶*1. The right to nationhood* [Pravo narodnosti] *and the rights of convenience* [blagoudobstvo].

The definition of the borders of a state as large and great as Russia is an important matter. The number of the different races[7] who, from East to West and from South to North, are subject to the great Russian nation and annexed to its state, is very great. One should not think of increasing their number or of extending [the state's] limits, but only strive to enthrone happiness throughout these extensive possessions. However, insofar, as the security of the state, and consequently its welfare, depends very much on good borders, it is no less necessary to examine the frontiers in detail and define them precisely.

If every state were composed only of one race or nation, its borders would be automatically defined by the area on which this people is settled, but as all great states, and more so Russia, encompass within their borders many different races, it becomes most

---

[7] Pestel' 's term is *plemia*, which in modern Russian means tribe. In the Russian Law it is used in the sense of race in the nineteenth-century definition of the term, or people, or tribe; it is here translated by any one of these, depending on the context.

difficult to define the boundaries. The difficulty arises from two contrary desires. Peoples subjected to a great state and of different origins than its dominant nation . . . want independence and a separate political existence for themselves: they base themselves on the right to form separate states and call this the *right to nationhood*. On the other hand, every large state strives to secure boundaries that are strong because of their location and natural defenses; at the same time it endeavors to have the power of the surrounding small nations increase its own might rather than that of some other neighboring big state: basing this striving and endeavor on its right to security, [the large state] calls it the *right of convenience*. . . .

Whether to favor the right to nationhood or the right of convenience must be decided on the basis of a third consideration: the right to nationhood exists in truth only for those nations which [not merely] enjoy it, but have the possibility of *preserving* it; while the right of convenience is taken into account to entrench security and not for the sake of a vainglorious extension of the state's borders. In this manner, the races which because of their weakness are subject to a larger state and cannot enjoy their own political independence, and consequently must necessarily submit to the power or protection of a large neighboring state, may not invoke the right to nationhood, for in their case it is fictitious and nonexisting. What is more, all small nations situated between big ones always serve as staging areas for military action, destruction, and all kinds of ruins and miseries. Therefore, it will be better and more beneficial to them if, spiritually and institutionally, they unite with a great state and merge their nationality completely with that of the dominant people to form one nation and stop dreaming uselessly of what is impossible and never to be. A strong state based on a great nation must always remember that Providence has not given it power for the oppression of its neighbors, but for actions that are righteous and in accordance with true justice. . . .

From everything that has been said here it follows that in order to set up borders correctly and positively, it is absolutely necessary to be guided by the [following] consideration: the right to nationhood must prevail in the case of those peoples who can enjoy their own political independence, whereas the right of convenience must prevail over those nations that cannot themselves make use of their political independence and must of necessity come under the power of some stronger state.

¶2 *Division of foreign peoples into those subject to the rule of convenience and those subject to the rule of nationhood.*

. . . Finland, Estonia, Livland, Courland, White Russia, the Ukraine, New Russia [*Novorossiia*], Bessarabia, the Crimea, Georgia, the entire Causasus, the lands of the Kirghiz, all the Siberian peoples, and other tribes living within the state have never enjoyed and never can enjoy their own independence; they have always belonged either to Russia itself or, at some time . . . , to Sweden, Denmark, Prussia, Poland, Turkey, Persia, or in general to some strong state. And in the future, too, because of their weakness, they will never be able to constitute separate states; for this reason they are subject to the right of convenience and must forever relinquish their right to be separate nations. . . .

As far as Poland is concerned, for many centuries it did enjoy complete political independence and constituted a large sovereign state. Even today it could exist as a power if it were to unite again into a common political organization all its constituent parts which powerful neighbors have seized. It follows from this that with respect to Poland the right to nationhood should, in strict justice, prevail over the right of convenience. And in truth it behooves the magnanimity of the glorious Russian people to grant independence to the fallen nation at the very time when Russia is securing a new life for itself. And thus, according to the rule of nationhood, Russia ought to grant Poland an independent existence. But the final determination of the borders between Russia and Poland must be left to Russia's right of convenience; and the reestablishment of an independent Poland must take place on such principles and under such conditions as to secure Russia fully against all future actions that might be detrimental to its safety and complete tranquility. . . . There are three principal conditions under which Russia should grant Poland independence: (1) The Supreme Power in Poland should be organized in the same manner as in Russia, on the basis of Chapter VI of the Russian Law. (2) The nomination and election of all persons and officials to all governmental and public offices in Poland should be on the same basis as in Russia, as provided in Chapters IV and IX of the Russian Law. (3) Any aristocracy, whether based on wealth and property or on privileges and hereditary rights, must be eliminated forever, and the entire Polish people, on the basis of Chapter IV of the Russian Law, must constitute a single estate. . . .

Attention should be paid also to some lands now bordering on Russia which must be annexed to Russia in order to establish firmly the security of the state. These lands are: (1) Moldavia; (2) lands of the Caucasian mountain peoples not subject to Russia and situated to the north of the Persian and Turkish borders, including the western coastal part of the Causasus which presently belongs to Turkey; (3) the lands of the Kirghiz-Kaisak nomadic hordes north of the mountain ridge, [extending] from the fortress of Bukhtarmin to the Sea of Aral: (4) a part of Mongolia, so that the entire course of the Amur River, from the Dalaia Lake on, belong to Russia. . . . The boundaries of Russia should not extend further than [these] limits.

¶3. *Defining the boundaries of the Russian state.*
//Systematic description of the boundaries of Russia.//

¶4. *The Russian state is one and indivisible.*

States may be *indivisible* [i.e., unitary] or *federal*. . . . At first glance, the federal organization of a state may seem more convenient and pleasant: for it gives to each region the possibility to act according to its judgment and will. But upon closer examination one becomes easily convinced of the decisive advantage of the indivisible [unitary] organization of the state over the federal. This is particularly applicable to Russia with its vast territory and great number of different tribes and peoples living in it. . . .

With respect to Russia in particular, it is enough only to recall the variegated elements that make up the vast state to be completely convinced of the harmful effect of a federal organization of the state. Not only are its regions governed by various institutions, judged by different civil laws, but their inhabitants are of different origin, speak completely different tongues, profess completely different religions, have at one time belonged to different powers. And if a federal organization of the state were to increase this variety further, one could easily foresee that these different regions will soon fall away from the Russian core; and Russia will then not only soon lose its might, greatness, and strength, but perhaps even its very existence as one of the principal great states. Then it will again experience all the miseries and unspeakable harm which had been inflicted on Ancient Russia by the appanage system, which was nothing but a kind of federal organization of the state.[8] Thus, if there are some states still in doubt as to the harm of a federal system, Russia cannot share this doubt at all: it has cruelly paid with bitter experiences and long-lasting miseries this error of its previous organization. And therefore . . . the Fundamental Law of the Russian state rejects any thought of a federal organization as utterly ruinous and evil. Everything that directly or indirectly . . . , overtly or secretly, could lead to such an organization of the state must be avoided.

On the basis of what has been said here, the Russian state, within the boundaries defined above, is declared *to be one and indivisible,* rejecting completely any federal organization, principle, or existence.

¶5. *Territorial division of the state.*

The territory of the Russian state is to be divided into fifty-three provinces, of which fifty are to be called areas [*okrug*] and three, "Districts" [*udel*]. Fifty areas form ten regions [*oblast'*] with five areas in each. The capital of an area or province in every region will also serve as the region's capital. The three "Districts" are to remain separate and not to be merged into any region; they are called: Capital, Don, and Aral ["Districts"]. Every region and "District" is to be divided into a varying number of districts [*uezd*] and each district into a varying number of townships [*volost'*].

. . . At the time of the original establishment of townships, particular care should be paid not to create overly populous townships. This is very harmful in many ways: the administration of the townships becomes very difficult; it is inconvenient for all citizens to

---

[8] Kievan Russia split into numerous independent and autonomous principalities from the thirteenth century until their absorption into Muscovy in the fifteenth century. In the eighteenth and nineteenth centuries it was commonly believed that the Mongol conquest and domination had been made possible by this splintering of Russia.

participate in the Land Assemblies, which will be mentioned later; agricultural work becomes more difficult as the distance between house and field increases. Moreover, large townships . . . resemble big cities; large cities, however, are particularly damaging to morality, which must be acknowledged the prime treasure of every nation. It is desirable [therefore] that at their inception the most populous townships do not exceed 5,000 to 10,000 individuals of the male sex. . . .

¶6. Selection and function of the capital.

The area in which the capital is located should not be part of any region, because the Supreme Administration with all the principal government authorities resides in the capital; and the union of the capital with any one of the regions will give the latter too much importance with respect to the others, and perhaps even [exercise] an influence on the affairs [of the state].

That is why the capital must be a separate area under the name of "Capital District." The province of Nizhnii Novgorod is made into the Capital District. . . . The city of Nizhnii Novgorod itself is made into the capital of the Russian state under the name of Vladimir. This name is given in memory of the great man who introduced the Christian faith to Russia; and let the name of Russia's center forever bear witness to the Russians' eternal gratitude for this pious and beneficent act. . . .

Nizhnii Novgorod has been chosen as the capital of the Russian state because: (1) this city is situated at the center of Russia; (2) located on the Volga and Oka rivers, it is, more than any other city, best suited for domestic trade and the supplying of all necessities in the large quantities required by a capital; (3) the Macarius Fair[9] connects Europe with Asia with respect to land transportation; (4) Russia's liberation from foreign domination by Minin and Pozharskii began in this city;[10] (5) all the antiquities of Nizhnii Novgorod

---

[9] Most important fair held yearly on the outskirts of Nizhnii Novgorod. It served as center of exchange for products of European Russia, Siberia, and the southeastern steppe regions.

[10] The movement of national liberation to free Moscow from the Poles was started from Nizhnii Novgorod by Kuz'ma Minin and Prince Pozharskii in 1612.

breathe the spirit of freedom and genuine love for the fatherland, but not for its tyrants.

The Provisional Supreme Administration pledges to take all measures and make all necessary appropriations for the establishment of the capital in Nizhnii Novgorod. Until then the capital is to remain in St. Petersburg or Moscow.

¶7. *The Don and Aral "Districts."*

The Don District, or the so-called Lands of the Don Cossacks, must form a separate area, because the purpose of the institution of Cossacks is to furnish the Russian army with such a remarkable cavalry of irregulars as the Don Cossacks. For this reason they must have their particular organization, especially an administration and chiefs of their own, completely in accordance with the purpose of their existence; and, consequently, [they must] be separate from the other areas of the state. . . .

//¶¶8-18. *Description of each of the ten areas into which Russia is to be divided.*//

Chapter II: *Of the Races Inhabiting Russia*

¶1. *Division of the races inhabiting Russia into three main categories.*

The general mass of the inhabitants of Russia may be divided into three main categories. The first category consists of the native Russian people; the second of races annexed to Russia; the third of foreigners living in Russia. The native Russian nation is a Slavic race. The peoples annexed to Russia consist of various other races. The foreigners living in Russia are private individuals from various nations. . . .

¶2. *The laws must be the same throughout the entire territory of the state.*

From a political point of view the state must form a *unit* . . . and it may be considered such only if its various parts and members are united by a strong and truly fast mutual bond. . . . It is, therefore, useful for the good and greatness of the state that the same laws and the same form of government prevail over all of its territory. It is only necessary to examine whether such a uniformity can exist. . . .

Religious laws may be divided into Christian law and others. The acts of all non-Christian faiths which are contrary to the spirit of the Christian law must be prohibited, but everything that is not contrary to its spirit, even though different from it, may be permitted according to circumstances. The Christian law possesses the same spirit in all its various denominations, and it demands from political laws only that they defend it and be in accord with this spirit. This is a requirement that must be fulfilled everywhere and there is no reason why it could not be applied everywhere uniformly throughout the entire territory of the state. It follows from this that variety in the religious laws may be combined with uniformity in the political laws and statutes. . . .

Finally, the political and civil laws may be uniform throughout the whole territory because: (1) Being a moral or theoretical truth, political truth is everywhere the same. (2) The peoples' customs everywhere depend on their religion and government. The precepts of Christianity require the same precepts of morality in all places, and a government with uniform political laws consonant with faith will help faith to introduce this holy uniformity of moral precepts for the sake of happiness for all, everywhere. (3) Justice does not permit ambiguity and ambivalent interpretations, and as it is based on an understanding of our obligations toward our neighbors, it must be the same in all places, the more so since faith defines these obligations in the same way for all men. And finally, (4) political laws are the nation's most effective teachers: they form and, so to speak, educate the people and it is from them that the customs, habits, and conceptions receive their characteristic traits and forms of action. They are the source of the orientation [given to] minds and wills and, therefore, one can positively say that it is political and civil laws which make the nations what they are. . . .

¶3. *Of the several varieties of the native Russian people.*

The Slavic race constituting the native Russian people comprises five "varieties":[11] (1) those actually called Russians, inhabiting

---

[11]Pestel' 's term is *ottenok*—literally, shade. It should be noted that Pestel' 's classification of the Eastern Slavic groups of European Russia is highly arbitrary by any objective criterion of language, religion, customs, or history.

the Great Russian provinces: (2) the Little Russians, living in the provinces of Chernigov and Poltava; (3) the Ukrainians, inhabiting the provinces of Kursk and Khar'kov; (4) the inhabitants of Kiev, Podolia, and Volhynia, who call themselves *Russnaks* [*Ruthenians?*], and (5) White Russians, inhabiting the provinces of Vitebsk and Mogilev. . . . There are differences in the present political condition of these provinces, but they will be replaced by a new statute which will improve their condition, and this prospective statute will be the same for all provinces. . . . From this it follows that there are no genuine differences between the several varieties of the native Russian people and that the small shades of difference that have been noted must dissolve in one common form. Therefore, the rule is to be established that all the inhabitants of the provinces of Vitebsk, Mogilev, Chernigov, Poltava, Kursk, Kiev, Khar'kov, Podolia, and Volhynia are to be considered native Russians and not [to be known] by any particular name.

¶*4. Of various races annexed to Russia.*[12]

The peoples constituting the various races annexed to the Russian state and living in it may be divided into ten categories: (1) Finns, (2) Letts, (3) Moldavians, (4) colonists settled in Russia, (5) nomadic peoples, (6) Tatars, (7) Caucasian peoples, (8) Cossacks, (9) Eastern Siberian peoples, (10) Jewish people.

As far as colonies are concerned, Russia has none other than those in North America, which are so unimportant that there is no point in much discussing them. . . . The general rule with regard to colonies is that they should be so governed that they can be granted independence if they are strong enough to make use of it; and, therefore, they should be ruled now more like protectorates then outright possessions.

¶*5. The Finnish race.*

. . . Experience has proven the ease with which Finland may become a genuine part of Russia. Adding to this consideration the definite rejection of any federal organization and consequently the establishment of political uniformity, the Supreme Administration pledges itself to introduce to all parts of Finland the same laws and

---

[12] Pestel' 's classification and description of non-Russian peoples is quite arbitrary and "unscholarly," even by the standards of his time.

administrative procedures that will be prepared for the Russian provinces. To Finland this order of things will be more useful and pleasant than the existing Russian and Finnish one. With respect to language, the Russian language should be introduced into Finland by establishing the necessary schools and taking all required measures as the Provisional Supreme Administration will see fit.

¶6. *The Lettish race.*

The Lettish race consists of two groups: the first are the Latvians, the second, the Lithuanians (or *Liakhi*).

The inhabitants of the provinces of Estonia, Livland, Courland are divided into two types: the native inhabitants and the newcomers. The native inhabitants are the Lettish people, who from time immemorial have settled in these places. The newcomers are the Germans, who have invaded these lands and divided among themselves the property and persons of the people conquered by them. . . . And the Provisional Supreme Administration pledges, therefore: (1) to pay great attention to the condition [of the Letts] and to the feudal system which has raged in Western Europe for such a long time and has pushed its rotten roots even here; and, (2) to take all measures for the complete and definitive eradication of the remainders of feudalism and for bringing the condition of the Letts into harmony with the fundamental rules that will serve as the foundation for the good organization of the state. And, therefore, the present political organization of these provinces must be replaced by the new order which will be established throughout the entire state. . . .

¶7. *The Moldavian race.*

The Moldavians inhabit the region of Bessarabia and the principality of Moldavia. The latter is to be acquired and annexed by Russia. Both Moldavian lands must receive the same organization that is proposed for all of Russia. All measures should be taken to offer these two regions the possibility of becoming completely russified and an integral part of one and the same whole, i.e., the Russian state. . . .

¶8. *Colonists settled in Russia.*

//The Provisional Supreme Administration should respect and implement the promises made to the colonists in the past; but at the same time give the lands settled by them the same organization that will be introduced in all of Russia; also equalize them in terms of civil rights, and introduce the Russian language.//

¶9. Nomadic peoples.

Nomadic peoples are of two kinds: (1) those living from cattle raising, and (2) those living from hunting and fishing. . . . The Provisional Supreme Administration has the sacred duty to give thorough consideration to [the condition of] these peoples. They are half savages, and some are even complete savages; they are peoples who do not know their own advantage and live in ignorance and degradation. Consequently, even out of a sense of Christian duty one should endeavor to improve their condition, the more so when to this reason we add the circumstance that they live in our state, in our fatherland. They should, therefore, become our brethren and cease stagnating in their pitiful condition. This goal would be largely attained if one succeeded in settling them permanently and turning them to agriculture. But this cannot be effected by direct measures; it is necessary to bring them this result indirectly. . . . Details of the steps to be taken to this effect, involving the distribution of land, the organization of public granaries and supply centers, imposing a uniform Russian administration. . . .[13]

As far as the *gypsies* are concerned, they should be given the choice of either leaving Russia or converting to Christianity, settling in the various districts, and merging into the general population. . . .

¶10 The Tatar race.

The Tatars found in Russia may be divided into three groups [Caucasus, nomadic, and all others]. With respect to the latter [e.g., Volga Tatars], the following three conditions obtain:

1. They profess Islam. They are allowed to keep this faith and any persecution of it is forbidden. Nonetheless, one should take advantage of all opportunities, through friendship and gentle exhortation, to persuade them to accept Holy Baptism; for this purpose it would be useful to consult with their religious leaders

---

[13] Pestel' is following here a line of policy that was introduced and quite successfully implemented in the great reorganization of Siberia undertaken by Speranskii in 1822. See M. Raeff, *Siberia and the Reforms of 1822* (Seattle: University of Washington Press, 1956).

2. They practice polygamy. But as this custom is contrary to the Orthodox Faith, it must be completely forbidden in the future. To keep women locked up is a great injustice vis-à-vis this half of the human race; therefore, gentle means should be used to have the Moslems give up this custom.

3. As the Tatars, and the Moslems in Russia in general, do not commit any unfriendly acts toward the Christians, it is only just to grant them all *particular* civil rights on a basis of equality with the Russians and to subject them to the same fiscal and personal obligations. . . .

¶11. Caucasian peoples.

The Caucasian peoples constitute a large number of separate possessions. They profess different religions, speak different languages, have different customs and systems of government, while their similarity consists only in one common predisposition to turbulence and robbery. . . . Considering that all previous experiences have unquestionably demonstrated the impossibility of turning these peoples to peace through friendly and gentle measures, the Provisional Administration is authorized to: (1) Conquer definitively all these peoples living in the lands north of the border that is to be established between Russia, Persia, and Turkey. . . .//After pacification, the peoples are to be given the same organization as Russia. The peoples who cannot be pacified are to be resettled in the interior of Russia, and Russians are to be settled in the Caucasus to russify this area.//

¶12. The Cossacks.

The Cossacks differ from other Russians not so much by their origin as by their way of life.//Details concerning their administrative reorganization.//

¶13. The Siberian peoples.

The peoples of Eastern Siberia are partly settled and partly nomads. The latter are subject to the same provisions as all the nomadic peoples in general. . . . In its concern for the improvement in these peoples' condition, the Provisional Supreme Administration must particularly keep in mind [the following]:

1. The dissemination and strengthening of the faith in a truly

Christian spirit will best contribute to the softening of [these peoples'] customs and to the introducton of enlightenment and education.

2. The creation of townships and the establishment of an administration on a common basis with Russia are the surest means for implanting order and happiness among these peoples.

3. Continue devising ways for the introduction of agriculture; after the bad results in the past, better ways may be discovered now, especially if attention is given to the [growing of various] vegetables, particularly the potato.

4. The unhappiest peoples are those who are administered by the American Company.[14] The Company oppresses them, robs them, and does not care at all for their fate; for this reason these peoples must be completely freed from the Company.

¶14. The Jewish people.

The Jews live primarily in the provinces of White Russia, Ukraine, New Russia, and Lithuania, and are distinguished from all other peoples mainly by the fact that they always maintain incredibly close bonds, never denounce each other under any circumstances or in any situation, and are always ready for whatever can be profitable and useful to their community exclusively.//The causes for this state of affairs are religion and the rabbinical control over all facets of Jewish life; the consequences are as follows: absolute power of the rabbis; the material resources are put at the disposal of the whole community; the expectation of the Messiah makes the Jews consider this life as transitory; the tendency to monopolize and exclude others from the places and positions into which they manage to penetrate.//

Taking into consideration all these circumstances, one can clearly see that the Jews, so to speak, form their own, completely separate state within the state and, in addition, at the present time enjoy rights in Russia greater than do the Christians.

One cannot blame the Jews themselves either for maintaining

---

[14] The Russian-American Company was entrusted with the administration of the islands of Sakhalin and the Kuriles, as well as Alaska. See Semen B. Okun, *The Russian-American Company* (Cambridge, Mass.: Harvard University Press, 1951).

such close bonds or for enjoying the broad rights which the previous governments have granted them; nevertheless, such a state of affairs may not last any longer, for it has implanted in the Jews hostile attitudes toward the Christians and has put them into a situation that is contrary to the political order in the state. Two ways are open for the correction of this state of affairs. The first consists in completely changing it. . . . To this end the Provisional Supreme Administration may call together the most learned rabbis and the most intelligent Jews, hear their representations, and then devise such measures as will put an end to the aforementioned evils and replace them by a state of affairs fully in accord with the fundamental rules that are to be the foundation of the political edifice of the Russian state. If Russia does not expel the Jews, this ought to be even more of a reason for them not to be in hostile opposition to the Christians. While it extends its protection and favor to every individual, the Russian government must, however, above all see to it that nobody thinks of going against the political system and private and public welfare. The second method, which depends on special circumstances and the particular course of external events, consists in assisting the Jews in the establishment of their own separate state in some area of Asia Minor. To this end an assembly point should be set up for the Jewish people and some troops given in support. If all the Russian and Polish Jews would come together in one place, they would be over two millions. So many people in search of a country will have no difficulty in overcoming all the obstacles which the Turks may put up; and after traversing European Turkey they could cross over into Asiatic Turkey where, upon seizing sufficient territory, they could establish a separate Jewish state. . . .

¶15. *Foreigners—nationals and aliens.*

Foreigners residing in Russia and belonging to various nationalities may be divided into two classes: (1) nationals, and (2) aliens. . . . The first may either petition to become citizens on a par with Russians or be put into the second category. For the latter, although always hospitable to aliens, Russia may not permit them to own real estate, enjoy the political rights of Russian citizens, and enter government service. They may petition to become citizens. . . .

¶16. All races must merge into a single nation.

From the contents of this whole chapter it follows that in all its measures regarding the various peoples and races inhabiting Russia, the Provisional Supreme Administration must constantly aim at making them into *one* single nation and at dissolving all differences into one common mass, so that the inhabitants throughout the entire territory of the Russian state be *all Russians*. The various means tending to this goal may be divided into two types: (1) General and particular. The general means consist, first of all, in making the Russian language prevail throughout the entire territory of Russia.//(2) Separate names of the peoples are to be abolished and only the name of Russia to be recognized.//(3) The same *laws* and only one system of administration may exist in all parts of Russia, so that over the whole expanse of the Russian territory the political and civil relations display a single origin, uniformity, and unanimity. The experience of all periods and all states has proven that nations are everywhere what their governments and their laws have made them. . . . Concerning particular measures, they have been mentioned above in connection with each people and race. . . .

Chapter III: Of the Estates Existing in Russia

¶1. Enumeration of the estates existing in Russia.

There are many different estates, conditions, or classes of people in Russia. Each has its distinctive aspects and privileges, its specially defined advantages and limitations. In the present situation there are to be found up to twelve different estates in the nation. These are: (1) clergy, (2) nobility, (3) merchants, (4) townspeople, (5) state peasants, (6) free agriculturists, (7) military colonists, (8) soldiers' children, (9) peasants of noblemen, (10) household serfs, (11) peasants attached to factories, and (12) peasants attached to monasteries. . . .

¶2. Estates do not form a gradual hierarchy in government.

There has been much discussion concerning the necessity of gradual hierarchies in governmental organization; namely, should the theoretical political space separating the mass of the people from the supreme power be subdivided into various degrees, and should this hierarchy, starting from the popular masses, rise to the supreme power? The idea [of gradualness] is a perfectly correct one and such a system is necessary. The proper means for its introduction and establishment have only to be devised. People who love misrule have maintained that such a gradualness demands the division of the people into many estates, so that the lower estate has few rights and no power whatever, and that all estates above it have varying degrees of rights, privileges, and powers, depending on their remoteness from the people and proximity to the sovereign power. These rules are derived from the feudal system and their essence in no way corresponds to truth, because the existing estates do not form a gradual progression. In the state, gradualness must be brought about in such a way as not to burden the sovereign power with all affairs in the state without exception; these matters should be decided on the lower levels, with only a part of them rising to the sovereign power through the levels set up between the latter and the various institutions where these matters may be initiated. It is obvious, therefore, that if the estates were to serve for this gradual progression, affairs would be brought up from the peasantry to the townspeople for decision, from these to the merchants, from the merchants to the nobility, etc. But as this would be too unreasonable, such a system exists nowhere. . . . In short, in the state, gradualness is necessary; however, it is found not in the nation's estates, but in the governmental bureaucracy which always exists quite independently from the estates, for the official must possess talents, knowledge, and virtues which may be found in all estates and which are not the particular property of any one of them. . . .

¶3. *Aristocracy of wealth.*

The division of the nation into estates—each being exclusively concerned with agriculture, handicraft, or trade—has been completely rejected by political economy, which has incontrovertibly proven that every man, provided he is honest and law-abiding, must have full and complete freedom to engage in the type of enterprise from which he may expect the greatest advantage and profit for himself. Of course, the government ought to contribute by all means to increase the national wealth, but this support must consist of various legislative and auxiliary measures regarding the economy and not of assigning the population to [specific] kinds of enterprise. . . . In addition, it should be noted that estates constituted by assigning private individuals on the basis of their economic activities are unreasonable and harmful: as [these estates'] existence is based on wealth, [their members] fasten all their wishes and designs on money exclusively; not knowing of any difference between men except [in terms of] money alone, they consider that wealth confers prime dignity, topping all others; and by rendering the people frightfully prone to self-interest, they inevitably bring about a moral deterioration. . . .

The distinctive feature of the present century is the open struggle between the people and the feudal aristocracy, in the course of which there arises an aristocracy of wealth much more harmful than the feudal aristocracy. For the latter always would be shaken by public opinion and was, consequently, to some degree dependent on it, while the aristocracy of wealth finds in its wealth means for its own designs against which public opinion is completely helpless; and by these means, as has been said already, it completely subjects the whole nation. For this reason every right-minded government must not only forbid such a division of the nation [into estates], but even take all measures to prevent such estates, as by themselves have split from the nation, from becoming established and rooted; and *a fortiori* it is obliged to destroy them where they do exist.

¶4. *All must be equal before the law.*

All the estates mentioned above have been formed at different times and under various circumstances, and by dividing the nation into different classes they have created great differences and distinctions in the political condition of men belonging to one and the same state. These distinctions aim neither at a better system of government . . . nor at the most convenient means for attaining the whole nation's general welfare; but they aim exclusively at granting greater privileges to some people and of oppressing the mass of the nation for the selfish interest of a minority. . . . It follows from this that in the state all men without fail must be completely equal before the law, and any statute violating this equality is an intolerable abuse that must be eradicated without fail. . . . From all that has been said above it follows that the estates must be destroyed, that inside the state all men must form but a single estate which may be called civic estate, and all citizens of the state must have one and the same rights and all be equal before the law. . . .

¶5. The clergy.

At present the clergy is most unjustly considered a particular estate of the Russian state. . . . The clergy is not a particular estate, but a particular calling which has its occupations and duties. And, therefore, the clergy must be considered *part of the government*, and its most respectable part. It is a branch of the state administration, a division of the bureaucracy, and the closer the bond between the clergy and the laity, the happier the nation, the more prosperous the state. The clergymen themselves are officials and at the same time Russian citizens, like all officials who occupy any position in the state administration. . . . The black clergy [i.e., monks] should not occupy any functions in the ecclesiastical administration, except in monasteries, and should leave to the white [secular] clergy all administrative offices of the hierarchy. . . .[15]

//Monks should lead a life in accordance with their vows, i.e., have no worldly interests; access to their ranks should be limited to mature individuals; the monks' missionary activities should be encouraged. Good education and training for the clergy should be fostered in theological *lycées* connected with the universities. Parish priests should have some training in medicine. Present material conditions are very bad and the new political order should provide a decent material basis for the clergy, especially the parish clergy.//

¶6. The nobility.

[At present the nobility is an estate separated from the mass of the nation by virtue of special privileges.] (1) To own other men in property, to sell, pawn, give away, inherit men like things, to

---

[15] This is a criticism of the practice of drawing members of the hierarchy (bishops, archbishops) exclusively from the ranks of monks and abbots. The secular clergy in Russia was, in fact, composed exclusively of parish priests. Incidentally, Pestel''s notion that the clergy was part of the government bureaucracy was not very radical, for this is what the Russian clergy had been in fact since Peter the Great's reorganization of the administration of the Church.

use them according to one's own caprice without their prior consent and exclusively for one's own profit, advantage, and at times whim, is shameful, contrary to humanity, contrary to the laws of nature, contrary to the Holy Christian faith, contrary, at last, to the will of the Almighty Who has declared in the Scriptures that all men are equal in His eyes and that only their deeds and virtues make for the differences in them. And for this reason there can no longer be in Russia the right for one man to possess and call another his serf. Slavery must be definitively abolished and the nobility must forever, without fail, renounce the vile privilege of owning other men. . . . Destruction of slavery and serfdom is enjoined to the Provisional Supreme Administration as its most sacred and unfailing duty. If it does not endeavor with all its might to carry out this command in the shortest time, by the most energetic and effective measures, it will be called [to account] before the throne of the Almighty and to eternal shame. . . .

//The nobility should not be exempted from paying taxes on an equal basis with others. Punishment for crimes should be uniform for all, hence, the nobility should not be exempted from certain types of punishment to which other citizens are subject.[16] Nobles should be liable to military service on par with other citizens. The nobility should not have the exclusive right to public functions. [Status] of nobility and of all titles and ranks [should be] abolished.//

¶7. *The merchant class.*

The existing statutes concerning the merchants (who are considered a separate estate) show many injustices, contradictions, and abuses whose many obstacles and difficulties ruin trade. It is known that the best means to foster flourishing prosperity consists in granting *freedom* and in having the government pay attention to the national economy only for the sake of spreading the knowledge and information necessary for industry and general enlightenment, and for removing those obstacles that exceed private means. From this it appears that freedom is the prime necessity of the national economy. This freedom consists of three elements: (1) Every citizen, pro-

---

[16] The nobility was exempted from capitation and from corporal punishment.

vided he is honest and law-abiding, should have the right and permission to engage in any branch of the economy he has thought it best to choose. (2) Everyone should be free to engage in any [economic] enterprise, not only in towns and specified places, but also in villages of all kinds, and wherever he might wish. (3) Economic enterprise itself should be freed, to the maximum extent possible, from all difficulties and obstacles which are the result not only of poorly conceived regulations but also of external actions and causes, in such manner that government decisions be not obstacles to the success of economic enterprise but, on the contrary, its protection and support. [Provisional Supreme Administration should take appropriate measures to secure economic freedom.]

¶8. Townspeople.

//Abolish their guilds and give them liberty to live and be active wherever they wish to; grant them the same civil rights as other citizens.//

¶9. Military colonists.

//System of military colonies is condemned as cruel and ruinous both to the government and the settlers. Military colonies are to be abolished and the settlers transferred to the general category of peasants.//

¶10. Soldiers' children.

¶11. Free agriculturists.

//To be given uniform rights with inhabitants of rural townships. May possess land individually or as part of communes, but the communes are not to possess more than one-half of the land in the township.//

¶12. State peasants.

//Free all state peasants and give them civil rights equal to those of all other citizens, so that they may become merchants and townspeople. Set up rural townships with one-half of the land in communal possession (not to be alienated) and one-half in the possession of the Treasury (which may sell it).//

First Draft[17]

Chapter III

¶*9. Peasants attached to monasteries.*

//Monks should have no estates, hence all peasants on monastery land are to be combined with state peasants and subject to the same measures.//

¶*11. Peasants of noblemen.*

The condition of the peasants belonging to noblemen varies greatly. Those belonging to the best masters enjoy complete happiness. Those belonging to the most cruel ones are in deepest misfortune. . . . This proves the necessity of a statute that would force the bad landlords to follow the example of the good ones, improve the peasants' condition as much as possible, and secure it positively on firm principles and rules.

//To this effect, provincial assemblies of the nobility are invited to submit projects. The spread of education is a good foundation for the improvement of the peasant's lot.//

But as this important enterprise demands mature reflection and will lead to a great transformation in the state, only gradual steps can bring it to a satisfactory conclusion. . . .//Projects of provincial nobility to serve as guide and themselves be guided in turn by the following://

1. Freeing the peasants from slavery should not deprive the nobility of the revenue they receive from their estates.

2. This [act of] freedom must not give rise to agitation and disorders in the state; to this end the Provisional Supreme Administration pledges to display unmerciful severity against all who violate public peace.

3. The freeing of the peasants must lead to an improvement in contrast to their present condition and not merely give the appearance of freedom.

---

[17] Even more incomplete and rambling than the second draft. Only selected passages dealing with topics not treated fully in the second draft have been translated or summarized here.

¶12. Household serfs.

Household serfs are the most pitiful estate in the whole Russian state. [Nobility's provincial assemblies to furnish projects of reform.]

Conveniently two measures may be put into action here: The first consists in fixing the number of years of service to the master, upon the expiration of which the household serf becomes free. The second consists in fixing the sum upon payment of which the household serf also becomes free. . . .

¶13. Peasants attached to factories.

//To be replaced by free labor or by convicts. All peasants attached to factories are returned to their original peasant status.//

Chapter IV: Of the Nation from a Political Point of View

//4. Population is divided geographically into rural and urban townships of various sizes.//

//7. Three types of citizenship relations: (1) Political rights, defining relation between the citizens and the government and the people's participation in the government. (2) Civil rights, defining the relation between citizens (family, marriage, guardianship, etc.). (3) Personal rights, defining the actions and way of life of citizens (freedom of enterprise, freedom of the press, etc.). All Russian citizens must have equal enjoyment of private, civil, and political rights throughout the whole territory of the state.//

//10. The lands of the township are divided into two parts, one-half in communal ownership and one-half in private ownership. The communal land provides the minimum for the *subsistence* of every member; it belongs to the whole community and is inalienable. Private lands are for the creation of a *surplus.*//

//12. Minimum livelihood guaranteed not out of charity but as a right. It will prevent poverty and beggars.

Each township will constitute a political family in which every member finds not only refuge and security, but also protection of his property and livelihood.//

13. . . . Representative government has solved the great problem of state administration and has reconciled the impossibility for

all citizens to gather together in one place with the unchallenged right of everyone to participate in government affairs. . . .

14. . . . The Provisional Supreme Administration is charged with the unfailing duty to [introduce] a representative system and to eliminate completely even the shadow of any aristocratic order, whether the latter be based on feudalism or on wealth . . . , so that nothing may hamper the citizens' choice and that they need not pay attention to either estate or property, but exclusively to talent and merits, and be guided by their confidence in those whom they have elected.

15. Therefore, the People's Assemblies [*narodnoe sobranie*] are to be divided into two kinds, the Land Assembly [*zemskoe sobranie*] and the Assembly of the Vicegerency [*namestnoe sobranie*]. There will be one Popular Land Assembly in every township, consisting of all the citizens in that township . . . and exclusively engaged in electing citizens to membership in the Popular Assemblies of the Vicegerencies, solely on the basis of confidence in the elected citizens. The Popular Assemblies of the Vicegerencies are to be concerned with all matters designated for popular participation and to consist of three degrees, so that every township has its Vicegerential Township Assembly, each district its Vicegerential District Assembly, and each area or province its Vicegerential Area or Provincial Assembly. . . .//Each Land Assembly will designate all its members to the membership of the Vicegerential Township Assembly and some of its members to the Vicegerential District and Provincial Assemblies.//

16. . . . The fear that the so-called populace will shake the state if it participates in the elections is completely unnecessary and groundless. The populace creates disorders only when it is oppressed or when the rich bribe and agitate it for their own ends; by itself it remains always peaceful. . . .

Chapter V: Of the Nation from a Civil Point of View

//On family, marriage, guardianship, inheritance, property rights, contract, personal freedom, fiscal obligation—in short, a skeleton civil law code.//

//13. Every citizen has the right to occupy any function in the public service. The rules of service are fixed by law and equally applicable to all citizens. The area of competence and jurisdiction of every office is determined by law.//

//14. Duty to obey the law, but not orders of individual persons. Nobody has the right to take the law into his own hands.//

//15. Establishment of universal military service.//

//16. The government has the duty to establish public institutions of education. Parents have the choice of educating their children in them, or privately.//

18. . . . (1) Every citizen has the right to write and print everything he wants, provided his name appears on his composition. Exception is made for personal insults, which should never be permitted. (2) Every citizen has the right to possess a printing press, provided he informs the government in advance and that everything he prints bears the name of the owner of the press. (3) Every writer is held responsible for the opinions and principles he expresses on the basis of the general laws against the dissemination of what is unlawful and immoral. . . .

19. . . . (1) The Christian Orthodox Graeco-Russian religion must be recognized as the ruling faith of the Great Russian state. (2) All other Christian denominations, as well as non-Christian faiths, are permitted in Russia, provided they are not contrary to the Russian spiritual and political laws, the rules of morality, and provided they do not violate the natural obligations of man.//Respect for all rituals of any faith and denomination. No one may interfere in the personal beliefs and dogmas of faith, which are matter of the individual's relationship to the Supreme Being.//

//20. Freedom to engage in economic activity for all citizens alike. Right to form corporations and companies. The government has the obligation to prevent formation of monopolies.//

//21. Establishment of banks and insurance companies by the townships.//

//22. The townships are to establish public granaries and the citizens are to inform the government of all changes and events affecting the normal course of trade and supplies.//

//28. [sic] and 24. General rules for public institutions of welfare and charity (orphanages, etc.).//

VI

The Society
of United Slavs

◄══◆══►

The officers of the regiments garrisoned in the southwestern borderlands of the Russian Empire tended to come from the poor gentry. All their lives they lived in proximity to the common people in their provinces of origin and military garrisons. They did not have much of an education; rarely, if ever, had they been abroad. These circumstances made them, unlike their more fortunate brethren in the capitals, more aware of the distinctive traits of the several nationalities in southwestern Russia. At the same time they were not given to look far afield for inspiration when considering an improvement and transformation of the conditions they knew from direct experience. In 1823, in the Ukraine, a small group of such officers banded together under the name of Society of United Slavs in order to work for the unification of all Slavic peoples. Their knowledge of the Slavic peoples outside of Russia were of the haziest (some even included the Magyars among the Slavs!), and much of what they knew they had learned from Polish sources. Besides being concerned with Slavic unity, they also felt deeply for the peasant and hoped to improve his lot by reviving what they believed to have been the Slavs' original native institutions.

The Society of United Slavs never elaborated a comprehensive plan of action or even a theoretical program. All that has remained of them is an oath for the members (a rather adolescent document), and a few very vague rules. No wonder that, when in 1824 they came into contact with members of the Southern Society at the military camp of Leshchin (where all the regiments stationed in southwestern Russia had been concentrated for maneuvers), they easily succumbed to Murav'ev-Apostol's and Pestel' 's intellectual and organizational superiority. They merged with the Southern Society, took part in the Chernigov mutiny, and shared the fate of their antinationalist, centralist associates.

Rules of the United Slavs by Petr Ivanovich Borisov
From *Vosstanie Dekabristov,* V (1926), 12-13.

1. Do not depend on anyone but your friends and your (weapons).[1] Friends will help you, (weapons) will defend you.
2. Do not wish to own a slave when you yourself do not wish to be a slave.
3. Everyone will consider you to be great if you cease to flatter pride and wealth.
4. Simplicity, sobriety, modesty . . . defend your peace.
5. Do not wish for more than you have and you will be independent.
6. Let the goddess of enlightenment be your domestic deity, and contentment and love will settle in your house.
7. Honor the sciences, arts, and crafts. Raise your love for them to a passion and your friends will genuinely respect you.
8. Let ignorance, with its children—pride, vanity, and fanaticism—be your evil spirits and devil.
9. Be tolerant of all religions and customs of other peoples; you are obliged to follow only the truly good ones.
10. Endeavor to destroy all prejudices, particularly those concerning differences in condition, and you yourself will become a man when you begin recognizing man in another human being.

---

[1] In the original manuscript the word weapon is indicated by a symbol.

11. If you are virtuous, the virtue of an entire lifetime will twist a wreath of peace to your conscience.

12. Even if you make use of your weapons when required to defend innocence and injustice, you will not be destroyed by vengeance, for friends will protect you.

13. If you assist your friends with your mind and weapons, they will help you in the same manner.

14. If you are such [a man], tyranny's pride and vanity will bend knees before you.

15. You are a Slav, and on your land—on the shores of the four seas that bound it—you will build four fleets (Black, White, Dalmatian, Arctic) and . . . you will erect a city where, through your might, you will enthrone the goddess of enlightenment. From there you will secure for yourself justice, to which you must submit, for it will not swerve from the road you have traced for it.

16. In your ports the Slav will prosper and so will trade and naval power, and rightness will reside in the city at the center of your lands.

17. If you want all this, unite with your brethren from whom your ancestors' ignorance has separated you. Do you wish to have all this, sacrifice one-tenth of your entire annual revenue and you will live in the hearts of your friends.

[The following in French.] You ought to observe that the spirit of servitude appears naturally arrogant, while the spirit of freedom is energetic, and that of true greatness is simple.

Oath of the Society of United Slavs
by Petr Ivanovich Borisov and Julian Liublinski
From *Vosstanie Dekabristov*, V (1926), 17-18.

Entering the ranks of the United Slavs to liberate myself from tyranny and to recover the freedom which is so valuable to mankind, I solemnly swear on this weapon to the mutual love which is my god and from which I expect the fulfillment of all my wishes. I swear always to be virtuous, eternally faithful to our goal, and to maintain the deepest secrecy. Hell itself with all its horrors will not compel me to inform the Tyrant on my friends and intentions. I swear that my lips will reveal the name of this Union only to the man who will have proven his indubitable desire to be a member; I swear to help you, my friends, from this sacred moment to my last drop of blood, to my last breath. My first virtue will be outstanding activity, and mutual love and assistance my sacred duty. I swear that nothing on earth will be able to affect me. With sword in hand I shall attain the goal set for us. I shall go through deaths, a thousand obstacles, and I shall dedicate my last breath to the freedom and the brotherly union of the noble Slavs.

If I should violate this oath, let remorse be the first avenger of my vile perjury; let this weapon turn its point against my heart, and fill it with hellish torments; let the minute of my life that was harmful to my friends be my last minute; let the minute of perdition when I forget my promise turn my existence into a succession of unheard-of disasters; let me be witness to the death in horrible torments from this weapon of everything dear to my heart and let this weapon strike me, the criminal, and cover me with wounds and shame, and after gathering on my head the full burden of physical and moral ills, let it stamp on this forehead the seal of Nature's miscast son.

[*The Aims of the Society of United Slavs*]
by Ivan Ivanovich Gorbachevskii
From I. I. Gorbachevskii, *Zapiski, pis'ma,*
B. E. Syroechkovskii, L. A. Sokol'skii, I. V. Porokh, eds.
(Moscow: 1963), pp. 13-14.

The society's main goals were: the liberation of all Slavic tribes from autocracy; the destruction of the national hatreds existing between some of them; and the unification of all the lands inhabited by [Slavs] in a federal union. The intention was to fix with precision the boundaries of every state; introduce a democratic representative form of government in each; establish a Congress to administer the affairs of the Union and to change, in case of need, the common fundamental laws, [while] leaving to the independent care of every state its internal organization and its particular legislation. In considering the principles on which rests the happiness of every private individual, we acquired the conviction that they were of a physical, moral, and intellectual [nature]. Therefore, civil society as a whole, composed of [single] units, necessarily rests on the same principles; and to attain the maximum possible happiness it requires: (1) industry to ward off poverty and want; (2) morality to correct evil inclinations, soften passions, and instill a love for man; (3) enlightenment—the surest companion in the struggle against the evils which are inseparable from [human] existence and provider of greater intelligence and know-how in all enterprise. The first and immutable duty of a Slav was to develop and disseminate these three main foundations of the common good. To the extent possible, he had to destroy prejudice and evil inclinations, eliminate class distinctions, and eradicate religious intolerance. By his own example he had to encourage temperance and industriousness, strive toward intellectual and moral perfection, and encourage others to it; assist the poor by all means available, but not be extravagant; instead of making people wealthy, he was to teach them how to make use of [their] riches through work and thrift without harming themselves or others.

Convinced of [the truth of] these principles, the Slavs were driven to the following conclusions: no revolution can be successful without the consent and cooperation of the entire nation; first of all, therefore, the people had to be prepared for a new form of civic life before it was given to them. There is no other way for a people to be free but first to become moral, enlightened, and industrious. Although military revolutions reach the goal faster, their consequences are dangerous: instead of being the cradles of the liberty in whose name they are made, they become its coffin. Persuaded that their hopes could not be fulfilled as fast as they would have liked, the Slavs did not want to waste time in empty and impossible efforts; but they decided to do everything in their power which would lead, albeit slowly, to the proposed goal. In execution of this enterprise they decided: to set aside a specified share of the common funds to purchase the freedom of serfs; to attempt or foster the establishment of small village schools; to instill peasants and soldiers with a need for knowing the truth and a love for the performance of civic obligations; and to stimulate in this way a desire for . . . ;[2] and to change the demeaning condition of slavery, etc.

However, in spite of these gradual and gentle measures, the Slavic Union was also militant.

---

[2] The ellipses are in the document. Some scholars have argued that they stood for freedom or liberty, but that reading has been contested by others.

VII

Investigation,
Trial,
Execution

By modern, Western standards, the investigation and trial of the Decembrists was hardly conducted dispassionately and fairly. However, it should be remembered that Russian judiciary procedure of the time did not know public trials and the give and take, argument and counter-argument between defense and prosecution. Cases were tried strictly on the basis of written testimonies, reports, and conclusions; the judges did not see the defendants until sentencing; the defendant could not do or say much beyond the testimony he gave before an investigating officer. In the light of these practices—from the government's point of view—the trial of the Decembrists was conducted according to the rules and in all fairness. Yet, the report submitted by the Supreme Criminal Court to the Emperor gives the impression of being very defensive. It seems that the Court was trying to compensate by sophistical, bureaucratic casuistry for the fundamental inadequacy of their procedures. The report also provides a curious illustration of the belief held by most prominent statesmen in Russia at the time, that manipulating procedures and devising elaborate categories and definitions were tantamount to concrete and positive reform. The Court's work, and the drafting of its report, was directed by a virtuoso of the bureaucratic style, the moderate M. M. Speranskii, who seems to have wanted to salve his own conscience while displaying zeal in the performance of this unsavory task. It should be added that Emperor Nicholas kept a very close watch over all phases of the proceedings. He participated in the preliminary examinations of the accused himself; he received daily reports on their behavior; he determined the prison regime for each individual prisoner; finally he gave precise instructions to the Court.

All these circumstances taken together gave the proceedings the aspects of a "kangaroo court." And if the final sentences were not extremely harsh by "normal" standards (after all, the Decembrists had taken up arms against the State), they were almost universally considered cruel and highly unjust because of the way the accused had been treated.

The descriptions of A. Murav'ev and B. Shteingel' not only give a fairly accurate picture of the actual circumstances of their own imprisonment and of the execution, they also convey something of the psychological and emotional impact of these events. They help us to understand how unprepared the Decembrists had been for what happened after the failure of their rising—mainly because they had never felt truly guilty, and they had never believed that their actions were in any sense criminal, since they were directed solely to the better good of Russia. Last but not least, the selections explain the origin of the notion of the Decembrists' "martyrdom"— a legend the Decembrists themselves helped to create through their memoirs.

Mon Journal by Alexandre [Mikhailovich]
Mouravieff [Murav'ev]
From Theodor Schiemann, *Zur Geschichte der Regierung Paul I und Nikolaus I,* 2nd ed. (Berlin: 1906), pp. 171-76.

The fortress of St. Petersburg, hideous monument of absolutism, faces the Monarch's palace, like a fateful warning that the one can exist only because of the other.

The habit of having before one's eyes the dungeons where moan the victims of arbitrariness must, in the long run, necessarily dull pity for one's neighbor's suffering. Great God! When will the day come when it will be understood that men have not been created to be the toys of a few privileged families. When the sun of publicity shines on Russia, the iniquities hidden by these walls will make one shudder.

There were not enough cells for the great number of victims. Buildings that had served as barracks for garrison soldiers were transformed into prisons. The window panes, covered with a layer of chalky paste, prevented the invigorating sun from penetrating into these lairs. In the long rooms of these barracks they had built cages with beams spaced in such a way as to prevent any communication. The prisoner could make only two or three steps along the diagonal of his cell. . . .

We arrived [from Reval], passed the drawbridge, stopped at the door of the Commandant's house. The *fel'dieger*[1] turned me over to the Major, who, without speaking a word to me, led me to a dirty, humid, dark, and narrow cell. A broken chair, an ugly pallet, and a chain of iron sealed by one end to the wall were the only furniture. After a trip of 360 versts[2] covered at top speed, after months of confinement, I was broken with fatigue. After the old Major had gone, I threw myself completely dressed on the horrible pallet. . . . Here I was, alone, separated from the living. I spent hours lying down, thinking of my mother, of my brother who, I knew, was held in the same fortress. Tears came to my eyes; I prayed to God and the prayer comforted me. A feeling of joy penetrated my soul. I felt proud to share the fate of my excellent brother. Taking courage, I rose, walked in my cell. Suddenly, I heard again the noise of locks, of my doors. The Major reappeared and took me to the Commandant of the St. Petersburg fortress, General Sukhin, an old veteran whom I had known as a child. He received me seated at his desk, pretending not to recognize me, and asked for my name. I answered that I was called Murav'ev and that I was an officer of the Cavalier Guards. To this he thought it polite to say: "I am quite sorry for the memory of your esteemed father who has a criminal in you." I shook on hearing this, but a sentiment of pity seized me at the view of this poor old man who was so dulled by servility

---

[1] *Fel'diegers* were special couriers on orders of the Emperor or central government authorities.
[2] A verst is 3,500 feet.

that he could remain completely indifferent to the sight of someone's sufferings, of someone who did not share his views. After the interview I again found myself in my cell, but this time I was happy to be alone. I remained in my cell deprived of light, without food, almost for eight days. In the morning, a jailer accompanied by a guard brought bread and water. One morning the doors of my cell opened at an unusual hour. This time it was General Stukulov, whom I also had known previously. He behaved like a gentleman, sighed to see me, with tears in his eyes he asked about my health . . . and whether I had heard from my mother and then left me. Once a month the Emperor sent one of his general *aides-de-camp* to visit the prisoners to show that he took a lively interest in their fate. This veil of concern hid the desire to find out the prisoners' convictions and at the same time bewitch our poor relatives.

The food was terrible, the money provided for our upkeep was pilfered by the employees, the old Major at their head. Some of the prisoners were on bread and water. Many had irons on their feet and hands. It was the Emperor himself who . . . prescribed the diet as well as the painful aggravation of a harsh captivity. Moral tortures were tried too. Prisoners sometimes received heartrending letters from their unfortunate relatives who, fooled by appearances, fulsomely praised the magnanimity of him who had never shown it. A priest had to bring the consolation of religion and above all provoke confessions. After he had come to know us better, he confessed the error concerning us into which he had been led. The bloody denouement of our trial surprised him and provoked his lively indignation. Many prisoners became ill, several lost their minds, some attempted suicide; Colonel Bulatov let himself starve to death.

The Committee of Investigation[3]

The Committee was composed of the Minister of War, an inept old man who filled the president's chair; Grand Duke Michael, who found himself both judge and a party in his proper cause; General Diebitsch, a Prussian who, like so many other foreign adventurers, enjoyed the sovereign's favor; General Kutuzov, Gover-

---

[3] Its official title was Investigating Commission.

nor-General of St. Petersburg; Prince Golitsyn, formerly Minister of Religious Affairs; Generals Potapov, Levashev, and Chernyshev. Colonel Adlerberg, *aide-de-camp* of the Emperor, was present to take notes which he submitted to his master daily.[4]

This inquisitionary tribunal met in the house of the Commandant of the St. Petersburg fortress. In the beginning it met during late night hours; later, when they were hastening to finish our trial, the meetings took place day and night. During the night sessions the prisoner was brought before his judges prepared by fasts and suffering. The Major, or one of his *aides-de-camp,* came to fetch the prisoner in his cell, put a hood on his head before he left his cell, and taking him by the hand led him in silence through the halls and passageways of the fortress. Only in the brightly lit room where the Committee met was the hood removed. Without giving him time to collect himself, the Courtiers in resplendent uniforms put questions on which depended the life or death of the person questioned and demanded precise and quick answers concerning events completely unknown to the accused. His silence was considered a new crime with which he was charged.

For a guiding thread in such a complicated affair, the Committee had the two denunciations of Sherwood and Maiboroda, as well as the papers seized in the homes of the accused. This is how my brother's Constitutional Project came into their hands. It was more difficult for them to get hold of the project of Pestel', who had taken the precaution of burying in an unknown spot the fruit of many years' labor. Thanks to Maiboroda the Committee found out the spot. . . .

---

[4] Actually the membership of the Commission was as follows: General Aleksandr Ivanovich Tatishchev (1763-1833): Minister of War 1824-27, President; Grand Duke Mikhail Pavlovich (1798-1849); Prince Aleksandr Nikolaevich Golitsyn (1773-1844): Procurator General of the Holy Synod, and Minister of Religious Affairs 1803-24; Dmitrii Nikolaevich Bludov (1785-1864); General Pavel Vasilievich Golenishchev-Kutuzov; Aleksandr Khristoforovich Benkendorf (1783-1844): later was head of the Third Section; Vasilii Vasilievich Levashev (1783-1848): later was President of the Council of State; Prince Aleksandr Ivanovich Chernyshev (1786-1857): later was Minister of War and President of the Council of State. Vladimir Fedorovich Adlerberg (1790-1884) had been *aide-de-camp* to Grand Duke Nicholas and remained one of the new Emperor's closest personal friends.

This Secret Committee, as it was called, was like a tribunal of the Inquisition, without a sense of respect and consideration for humanity, without a shred of justice or impartiality, and with a profound ignorance of the laws. When it was gripped by the notion of finishing its task rapidly, it threw together pell-mell the guilty and the innocent, to finish up and have the merit of speed. All the courtiers, who had but one goal in life, the capture of their master's favor, refused to admit any political opinion differing from theirs. These men were our judges. Chernyshev and Levashev distinguished themselves most by their animosity toward us; both had set themselves up as the interrogators par excellence. All means were good to them. They assumed false testimonies, they had recourse to threats of confrontations which they did not grant. More than once they assured a prisoner that his devoted friend had admitted everything. The accused—obsessed, pressured without pity or mercy, in a stupor —gave his signature. The friend was brought into the meeting chamber. . . . The accused fell into each other's arms, to the great amusement of the Committee members. The accused, however, had signed their death sentences. Colonel of the General Staff Falenberg, morally deranged by his imprisonment, was led to accuse himself of intentions he had never had. His friend, Prince Boriatinskii, proved it to him in a succinct and logical way before the Committee. The Committee, disregarding the moral and mental derangement of Falenberg, greatly praised his repentence and sentenced him.

An officer of the Marine Guards, Divov, barely nineteen years old, whom prison and bad treatment had also deranged, accused himself of having had only one dream while in captivity: namely that he was stabbing the Emperor. The Committee had the impudence to turn this into a count in the indictment. I am mentioning only the most striking facts. It happened that these gentlemen of the Committee would say with a naïve joviality, "Confess quickly, you are making us wait, our dinner is getting cold."

The Committee had as a main goal to pass us off as regicides; this has thrown a veil of reprobation in the minds of the rabble, which neither listens nor thinks.

When asked about regicide, Colonel Lunin, well known for his wit and his daring character, answered, "Gentlemen, the Secret Society never aimed at regicide; its aim was nobler and higher.

But anyway, as you well know, the idea of regicide is not new in Russia; there are some quite recent examples of it." Two members of the Committee, Tatishchev and Kutuzov, had participated in the bloody death of Paul. [Lunin's] answer hit the target and the Committee was put out. The Committee insisted vehemently that Nikita Murav'ev confess that the Northern Society wanted a republic. Tired of so much persistance, Nikita Murav'ev answered: "My constitutional project which is in your hands is a monarchic one. But if you wish to know, study has confirmed the direction of my political ideas and today I declare it openly: I am a republican in heart and mind."

As soon as he returned to his cell, the prisoner received a visit from the priest. Members who were not much implicated amused themselves at fooling the Committee. Among others, Captain Gorskii, when asked why he had joined the Secret Society, answered "only to follow the fashion."

There were also comical scenes. Major Raevskii, a brilliant wit, speaking of the Germans made Diebitsch jump in his seat. Prince Shakhovskoi confessed nothing and still was sentenced to exile. Colonel Grabbe, known for the nobility of his character, and a very distinguished officer, questioned by Chernyshev refused to have him as his judge. He declared that during the campaign of 1814, he had vainly ordered Chernyshev to join him with his detachment during a skirmish with the enemy. Chernyshev had not wished to share the dangers of the battle and had been berated by Grabbe. Count Zakhar Chernyshev was convicted only because one of the judges carried the same name. Zakhar's grandfather had created a very large entail; General Chernyshev—not in the least related to the Marshal who had established the entail—had the arrogance to make claims against the property of a family that in all respects was alien to him.

Many individuals, very much compromised, were not even questioned. . . . M. Orlov was arrested, kept in the St. Petersburg fortress and released. The Committee of Investigation, appointed on December 17, 1825, went into session immediately and closed its labors on May 30, 1826. It transferred the matter to a High Court of Justice that dispatched it with all possible speed, for it judged and sentenced without seeing or hearing us.

The sentence was carried out twenty-four hours after it had been read to us.

Most Dutiful Report of the Supreme Criminal Court
From Iu. G. Oksman, ed., *Dekabristy—otryvki iz istochnikov*
(Moscow and Leningrad: 1926), pp. 432-41.

To the Most Serene, Most Sovereign, Great Lord, the Emperor and Autocrat of all Russia, from the Supreme Criminal Court a most dutiful report.

The Supreme Criminal Court, established by the Manifesto of June 11 of this year for judging the state criminals, most dutifully submits for Your Imperial Majesty's consideration the essence of the sentences passed on them, describing first the order of procedure followed in this case.

The procedure [to be followed] in criminal cases is set forth in general laws, but in the case of the highest crime of state the common criminal procedure is inadequate. Therefore, at the very inception of this court, Your Imperial Majesty deigned to give it additional rules based on general judicial procedure and necessary for the successful conduct of this case.

The Supreme Criminal Court opened its session on June 3 with a reading of the Imperial Manifesto, of the report of the Commission of Investigation, and of the detailed data on every accused prepared by the same Commission from its original files. Everything that had been fragmentarily known from previous information concerning these crimes emerged from the reading of these files as a comprehensive picture of all the circumstances. The more the Court entered into the details, the more the abyss of hatred and moral bitterness seemed to broaden. All previous feelings of horror and loathing were aroused with renewed force.

But the Court could not, should not, be swayed by these feelings. As it measured the crimes it still saw only defendants. However reliable the documents of the Investigating Commission, commonly [accepted] judicial procedure and the rules prescribed by Your Imperial Majesty demanded [their] confirmation through personal questioning. Two ways were open to this end: the calling of the accused before the Court or the deputizing of a commission selected by the Court from among its own members. Your Imperial Majesty deigned to leave the selection of either method to the discretion of the Court. The second method was chosen for being as sure [as the first] but more convenient in view of the number of defendants.

The Commission of Review fulfilled its assigned task precisely. All defendants, without exception, confirmed their previous testimony with their signatures. They were given opportunity to complement these testimonies [by mentioning] the circumstances they might think useful for their exculpation. Some, five exactly, took advantage of this opportunity and submitted explanations. And though the Commission found nothing in them of importance or essential significance, it submitted them nevertheless for the Court's consideration. . . .

After completing the review of the investigation, the Court proceeded to a reading of the laws concerning crimes of this kind. . . . In relating these laws to [the circumstances of] this case, there automatically arose the following two questions: (1) To what order of crime do the crimes revealed in the documents of the Investigating Commission belong? The Court decided unanimously that they all belong to crimes of state. . . . (2) What punishment is provided for these crimes by our laws? The Court recognized, and unanimously decided, that the crimes defined in the dossiers—and twice confirmed personally by the defendants—are without exception punishable by death.

With this single common sentence the case was closed according to the strict terms of the law. The severity of our laws does not permit distinguishing any degrees [of culpability] in crimes of this kind. All those who acted on, agreed upon, participated in, and even those who only knew of—but did not report—the design of assaulting the sacred person of the Sovereign Emperor or a member of the Imperial family, as well as of scheming a rebellion and military mutiny, were all without exception subject to capital punishment, and by virtue of the strict application of the law were deemed sentenced to such an execution by one common sentence.

The beneficent severity of our laws may be tempered by the Monarch's mercy alone, but tempered only in particular cases, in the form of a given and specific exception, not as a general rule of permanent force and application.

In consideration of which Your Imperial Majesty was pleased in this case to order graciously that the Supreme Criminal Court determine: "To what extent is the common guilt of the criminals increased or decreased by every person's particular and individual circumstances; and [that the Court] establish various categories or degrees of culpability, set a penalty for each one, and classify the defendants according to these categories and degrees." (Additional articles, part II, articles 3, 12, 13, and 14 [of imperial instructions].)

In execution of this sovereign command . . . a special commission was selected from among the members of the Court. Clearly, the principles of the categories had to be sought in the circumstances of the case. To this end two instruments were available: the report of the Investigating Commission and the dossiers of its work. In the report, the circumstances are set forth in their totality; in the dossiers they are presented in all their detail, with the answers of the defendants themselves, their very testimonies, written or signed by them, and twice—during the investigation and then during the review procedures—confirmed by them. The Commission deemed it just to combine the two instruments, i.e., coordinate and check the report of the investigation and review separately all dossiers from beginning to end. However complicated this task, it was a necessary one. By bringing it to completion the Commission acquired, in the first place, the opportunity of surveying the full extent of the case's details and of basing the categories not merely on the report but on the original dossiers; in the second place, the Commission convinced itself not only of the accuracy of the report and of its relationship to the dossiers, but also of the accuracy of the procedure. In a total of 121 dossiers, only six cases were discovered—and very minor ones at that—which required some clarification, and which, therefore, had to be complemented by the Investigating Commission. Although this did not affect the essence of the case, it clarified details.

Having reviewed the entire case in this manner, the Commission proceeded to establish the categories. For this it had to: define the main types of crimes, distinguish in every type all aspects, and after ordering them according to their degrees, derive . . . the principles for each category.

Types of crimes: From an over-all perspective, all the different parts of this vast affair represent one principal design: to shake the Empire, to destroy the basic laws of the fatherland, to transform the entire order of government. To accomplish this design three means, three main types of crimes, were suggested: (1) regicide, (2) rebellion, (3) military mutiny.

Aspects of the crimes: Every one of these three main types leads to its own long series of crimes: (1) knowledge of the design, (2) agreement with it, (3) appeal for its execution; but each of these aspects admits of various degrees. . . .

Principles for the categories: It is clear that in order to define the categories [of guilt] there is no other way but to relate, for every type of crime, these aspects to their seriousness. He who is guilty of all three types of crimes in combination with the first aspect of each must, without doubt, be put in the first place. After him follow those who have been found guilty of only two types (in combination with their first aspects), but whose guilt in the third is either less than the first or altogether lacking.

The Commission based the categories on this general rule, but in applying them to such diverse cases it was necessary to permit some qualifications. A very heavy guilt in one type of crime was in one person frequently combined with lesser guilt in the other types. But in the case of several crimes, the law determines the punishment on grounds of the most serious one [of them]. It was necessary to put this most serious crime in the relevant category, even though with respect to other crimes [the defendant] belonged to lower categories.

In view of the variety of crimes, the Commission sought above all not to mix up one type with another, not to leave out of consideration any significant difference, but to provide a place for every aspect and put it in its proper relation to the others. In this fashion there were derived eleven categories of crimes.

To verify their accuracy, the Commission decided that it was necessary to make a test by distributing persons according to them —a test, not the assignment itself, which belonged to the competence of the Court and which the Commission could not anticipate.

For this it was necessary, so to speak, to go over anew the history of each defendant. . . . In this manner was compiled a general roster of the defendants with a short, but precise, indication of their crimes. On the basis of these, the defendant's place and category were determined. This laborious procedure satisfied the Commission that the greatest number of defendants could be distributed among the categories with precision and with due regard to all essential circumstances. . . . The guilt was heightened by the serious consequences of setting an evil example, the destruction of military discipline, by bloody actions of wild cruelty. On the contrary, guilt was decreased by (1) signs of repentance . . . , (2) the defendant's particular deeds that also belong to a decrease in guilt, (3) rapid and complete confession during the investigation, (4) the defendant's youth at the time he was enthralled by the criminal society. . . .

//A few defendants' guilt exceeded that of all others. The Commission put them into a separate list.//

The Supreme Criminal Court, having examined the conclusions of the Commission in all detail, recognized by majority vote that the number of categories . . . corresponded to the variety and quantity of types of crimes. Thereupon, in fulfillment of the rules prescribed to it, the Court proceeded to set the penalty for each category. The Court could not depart from the general rule, unanimously accepted at the start, that in strict application of our laws all defendants without exception were deserving of capital punishment. Therefore, if on the basis of the categories of punishment it will please Your Majesty to grant to some [defendants] their life, it will be neither the law's nor even less the Court's action, but solely an act of the Monarch's mercy. It will be a special exception permitted for this case only by Your Imperial Majesty's decision. Although the law may put no limit on the mercy flowing from the Autocratic Power, the Supreme Criminal Court makes bold to submit that there are degrees of crimes so great and so closely related to the general security of the state that they should be inaccessible to mercy itself.

On the basis of these considerations, the majority of the Court decided to submit to Your Imperial Majesty's consideration the following statement of sentences and punishments:

1. For all criminals who by the special nature and seriousness of their crimes cannot be included under any category, death through quartering.

2. For all criminals belonging to the first category, the penalty of death through beheading.

3. All criminals in the second category are to be given what in our laws is called political death, i.e., lay their heads on the scaffold and then be sent to forced labor in perpetuity.

4. Criminals in the third category, after deprivation of ranks and nobility, are to be sent to forced labor forever.

5. Criminals in the fourth, fifth, sixth, and seventh categories, upon deprivation of ranks and nobility, are to be exiled to forced labor for a specified period and, upon completion of this period, to perpetual settlement [in Siberia].

6. Criminals in the eighth category, after deprivation of ranks and nobility, perpetually banished to settlement [in Siberia].

7. Criminals in the ninth category, after deprivation of ranks and nobility, are to be enrolled as soldiers, without [right to] promotion.

8. Criminals in the tenth category, upon deprivation of ranks and nobility, are to be enrolled as soldiers with right to promotion.

9. Criminals in the eleventh category are to be deprived of ranks and enrolled as soldiers with right to promotion.

. . . The 121 defendants are sentenced, by decision of the Supreme Criminal Court, as follows: five outside all categories to death through quartering; thirty-one in the first category to death by beheading; seventeen in the second category to political death and exile at hard labor in perpetuity; two in the third category to exile at hard labor forever; thirty-eight in the fourth, fifth, sixth, and seventh categories to hard labor for a specified period, and settlement; fifteen in the eighth category, after deprivation of ranks and nobility, to settlement for life; three in the ninth category, upon deprivation of ranks and nobility, to exile in Siberia in perpetuity; one in the tenth category, upon deprivation of ranks and nobility, enrolled as a soldier without right to promotion; eight in the eleventh category, upon deprivation of ranks, enrolled as soldiers with right to promotion. . . .

In conclusion, the Supreme Criminal Court has the duty to report that decisions and sentences were pronounced by a majority of the members of the whole Court or by a plurality of votes of the same opinion.

At the time of writing the final general protocol, in accordance with their rules and previous precedents, the members of the Supreme Criminal Court from the Holy Synod have expressed their opinion in the following words: "Having followed in the Supreme Criminal Court the investigation of the criminals of state, Pestel', Ryleev, and their other accomplices, who planned regicide and the introduction of a republican government into Russia, and seeing their own admission and complete unmasking, we agree that these criminals deserve the severest sentence. Consequently, whatever the sentence, we do not reject it, but inasmuch as we belong to the priesthood, we cannot sign the sentence."

. . . The Supreme Criminal Court, fully conscious of the solemnity of its assignment, wished to justify completely Your Imperial Majesty's trust, and in working with unflagging care through the complexities of this vast case it has sought only, in Your Own words, "justice, unbiased justice, unshaken by anything, founded on law and the force of evidence."

Memoirs by Baron Vladimir Ivanovich Shteingel' [Steinheil]
From V. I. Semevskii, V. Bogucharskii, P. E. Shchegolev, eds.,
*Obshchestvennye dvizheniia v Rossii v pervuiu polovinu
XIX veka*, Tom I: *Dekabristy—M. A. Fon-Vizin, kn.
E. P. Obolenskii i bar. V. I. Shteingel' (Stat'i i materialy)*
(St. Petersburg: 1905), pp. 459-61.

On the following day, July 12, the Supreme Criminal Court opened its last session in the Senate, having previously decided not to call the accused for sentencing into the Senate, but to go themselves to the fortress for this purpose. When all were assembled, the Metropolitan, in a short speech, pointed out the importance of the matter and proposed to find out "whether all have a clear conscience?" for there still is time to appeal to the Monarch's mercy. After receiving a positive reply, he said: "Let us pray then." All rose, crossed themselves, and went to the fortress in a long cortege of carriages accompanied by two squadrons of gendarmes. In the main salon of the Commandant's house everything was ready for the session. At the far end, tables covered with red cloth had been arranged in a rectangle, in the middle of which was a small table for the Chief Secretary and a rostrum for the Minister of Justice. This highest guardian of justice was Prince Dmitrii Ivanovich Lobanov-Rostovskii, well known for his passionate character that at times reached to rage; he was a good colonel in the time of Catherine [II] when the well-known rule concerning the posture of recruits was followed: "flog nine to death and have the tenth stand straight."

After the opening of the session all the prisoners were taken from the casemates and led through the back court and back portal into the Commandant's house.

The meeting of the prisoners, who for the most part had been held in solitary confinement, produced the strongest and most joyous impression. They embraced and kissed each other as if they had been resurrected, asking each other, "What does this mean?" Those who knew explained that the sentence would be announced. "Why, have they tried us?" "You have been tried already," was the answer. But the first impression was so strong that no one was much struck by this circumstance. All saw the end of a painful confinement.

. . . All were assembled and ordered according to their categories [of guilt]. Then, they were led in through one door and, after the reading of the sentence and its confirmation by the Chief Secretary, led out through another. There, in the next room, stood the Archpriest, Peter Myslovskii, everybody's consoler and confessor, with him a physician and two barbers with instruments for bloodletting. No one proved to need their philanthropic assistance, everybody was above the blow dealt to him. During the reading of the sentence, the judges showed no sign of pity, only curiosity. Some looked through a lorgnon as if at animals. It was easy to imagine what feelings this aroused in the accused. Lunin, who knew many of these gentlemen quite well, twisting his mustache laughed out loudly when his sentence of twenty years at hard labor was read to him. After the reading of the sentences everyone was put into another casemate.

On the night of the 13th, a gallows was erected on the glacis of the fortress, while the condemned naval officers were sent to Cronstadt. At 2 o'clock at night everything was in commotion in the fortress and near it. All the prisoners were led into the courtyard and ordered into two *carrés,* one for those who belonged to regiments of the Guard and the second for all the others. During this time Guard regiments took their stations around the esplanade. The morning was dark, foggy. Fires were lit near the *carrés*. At 3 o'clock the condemned were led out for the execution. In the second *carré* [the sentence] was carried out for all at the same time, in the first by regiments. . . . The epaulets and uniforms were torn off and thrown into the fire. Thus it was odd to see one [person] whose uniform and decorations had been left. This was Colonel Aleksandr Nikolaevich Murav'ev. They had forgotten to spare the witnessing of the execution to those who had been pardoned by the Emperor. When the second *carré* was led back into the fortress loud laughter was heard. Later this was ascribed to desperation and lack of feeling. But that was not at all the case. The object of laughter was Iakubovich who, wearing a plumed officer's hat, high boots, and a short dressing gown to his knees, stepped forth with comical seriousness.

The five victims,[5] who had not been allowed to see anyone prior to the announcement of their sentence, were led out in front of the troops with signs on their chests: "criminal, regicide." Beneath the gallows Archpriest Myslovskii took leave of them and blessed them. Pestel' came up to him last and said: "Though I am a Lutheran, Father, I am a Christian like the others, bless me too." After the hoods had been slipped on and the scaffolding taken away, as the martyrs hung with all their weight, three of them— Murav'ev, Bestuzhev, Kakhovskii—fell off.[6] One of the generals immediately rode up yelling, "faster, faster." In the meantime Murav'ev had had time to say "Oh Lord, they can't even hang properly in Russia." One must render full justice to the priest— we've named him. From the execution he carried away a profound feeling of respect for the martyrs. Without fear or hesitation he later told and wrote his friends that they had died like saints, he treasured the mementos they had given to him, and to the day of

---

[5] The five who had been put outside any category had their original sentence of death through quartering changed to that of hanging. These were: Pavel Ivanovich Pestel', Kondratii Fedorovich Ryleev, Sergei Ivanovich Murav'ev-Apostol, Mikhail Pavlovich Bestuzhev-Riumin, Petr Grigor'evich Kakhovskii.

[6] Witness accounts vary with respect to the three who fell off the gallows. The official report of the Governor-General of St. Petersburg named: Ryleev, Kakhovskii, and Murav'ev-Apostol.

his own death he remembered and prayed for the peace of their souls before God's altar. The bodies of the executed [men] were secretly taken to Golodai Island and buried there in secret.

This was the manner in which the execution of the unfortunate victims took place.

EPILOGUE

Russia's greatest poet, Aleksandr S. Pushkin (1799-1837), who had been close to many Decembrists, quickly perceived the historical significance of their lives and sacrifice. In a poetic message he offered it as a consolation and encouragement. Prince Aleksandr I. Odoevskii (1802-38), in his reply, shows how the Decembrists understood and accepted their historical role.

Message to Siberia [1827][7]
A. S. Pushkin

Deep in the Siberian mine,
Keep your patience proud;
The bitter toil shall not be lost,
The rebel thought unbowed.

The sister of misfortune, Hope,
In the under-darkness dumb
Speaks joyfully courage to your heart:
The day desired will come.

And love and friendship pour to you
Across the darkened doors,
Even as round your galley-beds
My free music pours.

The heavy-clanging chains will fall,
The walls will crumble as a word;
And Freedom greet you in the light,
And brothers give you back the sword.

---

[7] Translated by Max Eastman, in *Poems of Five Decades* (New York: Harper & Row, Publishers, 1955). Reprinted by permission.

Reply to Pushkin's Message [1827]
A. I. Odoevskii

The sound of your prophetic harp,
Impassioned, came to us at last.
Swiftly our hands reached for the sword,
But found that shackles held them fast.

Yet, singer, fret not: we are proud
Of these our chains as of our fate.
Locked in our prison cells, we scoff
At the rulers of the State.

Our grievous toil will not be lost,
The spark will quicken into flame;
Our people, blindfolded no more,
A new allegiance will proclaim.

Beating our shackles into swords,
Liberty's torch we will relight,
And she will overwhelm the Tsars,
While nations waken in the night.

(Translated by Valentine Snow)

Bibliography

I n English there is only one summary account of the Decembrist movement and revolt: Anatole G. Mazour, *The First Russian Revolution 1825—The Decembrist Movement: Its Origins, Development and Significance* (Berkeley, Calif.: University of California Press, 1937; reprinted by Stanford University Press, 1962).

The literature on the Decembrist movement in other languages (primarily Russian, of course) is immense. Two very complete bibliographies to it are available: (1) N. M. Chentsov, *Vosstanie Dekabristov—Bibliografiia* (Moscow-Leningrad: Tsentrarkhiv, 1929), covering the sources and materials from 1825 to 1928; and (2) M. V. Nechkina, ed., and R. G. Eimontova, compiler, *Dvizhenie—Dekabristov—Ukazatel' Literatury 1928-1959* (Moscow: Vsesoiuznaia knizhnaia palata, 1960).

Not included in these bibliographies are two recent works on partial aspects of the movement: Hans Lemberg, *Die nationale Gedankenwelt der Dekabristen* (Köln-Graz: Böhlau Verlag, 1963); and Georges Luciani, *La Société des Slaves Unis 1823-1825 (Panslavisme et solidarité slave au XIXe siècle)* (Bordeaux: Université de Bordeaux, 1963).

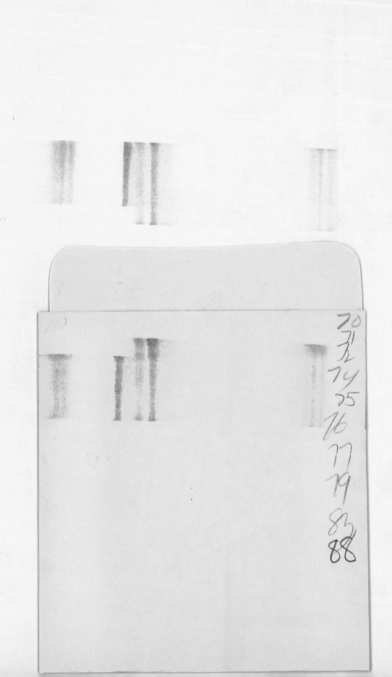

70
71
72
74
75
76
77
79
83
88